The Price

of

Being a Christian

Richard J. Hart

Fr. Richard

Wiseblood Books

Milwaukee, Wisconsin

Printed in the United States of America
Set in Arabic Typesetting

Edited by Joshua Hren
Cover Design by Sister Patricia Kolenda

Library of Congress Cataloging-in-Publication Data
Hart, Richard J., 1929—
The Price of Being a Christian
1. Hart, Richard J., 1929—
2. Popular Spiritual Writing
3. Social Justice—Catholic Social Teaching
4. Contemplation and Action
5. Inspirational Non-fiction

ISBN: 13: 978-0615821177
ISBN: 10: 0615821170

CONTENTS

FOREWARD

In his immense and often impenetrable *Finnegans
Wake,* in a terse, satirical, but mostly serious register, James Joyce
wrote that "Catholic" means "Here Comes Everybody." In *The
Price of Being a Christian,* Richard J. Hart makes Joyce's claim
manifest. Early in the book Hart makes a crucial observation:
though we hear much talk about the United States being
polarized, about the Church being *polarized,* we would speak
more accurately were we to call the current condition
tribalization. "The different tribes," Hart writes, include, "pro-life
Catholics, peace and justice Catholics, liturgical traditionalist
Catholics, church reform Catholics, just to mention a few. The
diversity can be a treasure but also create dysfunction, especially
when the tribes become each others' enemies." In order to
correct this dysfunction, we must build zones wherein divergent,
often viscerally oppositional "tribes" come together for the
common good of the Church and the world. The following pages
are, in part, an incarnation of this goal. For here we have the
unification of figures whose cloaks are often snatched and flown
as flags by one of the aforementioned tribes. We have *both* Pope
Emeritus Benedict XVI *and* Dorothy Day, Cesar Chavez *and*
Walter Cizek. Hart challenges us to recognize and respond to
both material *and* spiritual poverty, to recognize, in the words of
John Paul II, the "moral" dimensions of the ecological crisis, and
to, in the spirit of St. (and Pope) Francis, make life altering
decisions that will improve the state of God's creation. Indeed,
this work helps to restore our vision, so that by the end we will
see *one* holy, Catholic and apostolic Church instead of multiple
tribes.

Much of *The Price of Being a Christian* unfolds in the vein of Dietrich Bonhoeffer's *The Cost of Discipleship,* asking us at every turn to acknowledge the price Christ has paid, and the price we are asked to pay, in order to be Christian. Just as Bonhoeffer warned against "cheap grace," the belief that one can have forgiveness without contrition, communion without confession, grace without discipleship, so Hart beckons us away from the materialist, secularist temptation to avoid, at all costs, the sacrifices that are indivisible from our relationship with Christ. How often we are willing to pay a bit more at the store to receive a better-crafted, more reliable product. And yet how often we hesitate when we are asked to "pay" the price that would make us better-crafted Christians. Importantly, although Hart considers the very material, even monetary prices that every Christian should pay in order to fulfill the desires and commands of the God of justice, of the Christ of peace, he probes those prices which we are less likely to consider, of a spiritual economy that might seem like a scandal if our only reference point is the conventional one whose heart is located on Wall Street. For it is costly to defy the maxim *Time is Money,* to transcend this maxim with the understanding that *Time is God's.* For if Time is God's then we must pay the price of praying instead of arranging our lives exclusively around ways to make more money. When Time is God's, we operate according to an entirely converted set of values. We pay the price not of dollars and cents, but of hope in the face of hardship, of justice in the face of overwhelming economical disparities, of making suffering a window to the Lord rather than an obstacle. Ever-rooted in Scriptural revelation, Hart's faith that we can pay the price is placed not in our humanness, but in the One who, though he was in the form of God, did not fail to gain the Resurrection by laying down His life. Hart's work reminds us of the catholicity of Christ's call, as throughout the following pages he excludes no one from Christ's call to count not the cost of following. "Here Comes Everybody."

—Joshua Hren, Ph.D.

CHAPTER ONE
JESUS PAID THE PRICE

If anyone was willing to pay the price for us that person was Jesus. St. Paul wrote concerning Jesus, "though he was in the form of God, [he] did not regard equality with God something to be grasped. Rather, he emptied himself, taking the form of a slave, coming in human likeness" (Phil. 2:6-7). We follow Jesus' example by emptying ourselves and accepting our weakness as he did. Jesus was willing to become like us in all things but sin (Heb 4:15).

The Incarnation is not only a human event but also one that is a significant moment in salvation history. It is a meeting of heaven and earth. The Incarnation allows us to penetrate the impenetrable. It seems from his homilies that St. Augustine gave Jesus' Incarnation as much if not more emphasis than his Passion. The great saving mystery for him was the Incarnation, the fact of God lowering himself in humility to raise us up into dignity. St. John Newman asks what distinguishes Christianity from other religions, philosophies and ideologies. It is the Incarnation. God and man became one in the person of Jesus Christ. In asserting that Jesus took on our human flesh, we also assert that he accepted our

weakness, vulnerability and the messiness of our existence.
We cannot put aside Godhead and do what he did. In
accepting manhood Jesus did all the things a baby does—
drooling, spitting out food and a change of diapers.
Considering this mystery, Soren Kierkegaard called faith in
the Incarnation a commitment to the absurd because he
could not understand how Jesus could be God and man. It
is a mystery demanding much faith so it is not absurd. The
Incarnation means that we and God are in constant or
perpetual relationship. It is comparable to a four-year-old
telling his mother that "When I hug you, it's God hugging
you." That is a Hallmark moment!

Jesus came to us not as a powerful dictator, a
powerful athlete who was envied and admired, a rock star
who could make audiences swoon, but as a baby without
any power, and yet—he was God. We will never
comprehend the immensity of God becoming a little baby.
In his powerlessness he is more powerful than any king,
emperor, dictator, because through this act he touched the
hearts of many and will continue to do so. Jesus also died
powerless on the cross. That is why the crib and the cross
are intimately connected. St. Bernard of Clairvaux asked
the Lord what made him so small? The Lord responded
with one word: love.

Undoubtedly this was the greatest love story ever
written. When St. John put pen to paper he described it in
a few words, "The Word became flesh and made his
dwelling among us" (1:14). No romance novel will ever be
able to compete with it, not even the musical *Gone With*

the Wind, based on Margaret Mitchell's novel of the same name, which some consider one of the great love stories. Our problem is that God's love story is known too well and maybe has become threadbare like tires on a car. Once we grasp its fullness it makes us tremble and troubled because we often don't know how to return it. We can only return, however, by being renewed by the heartbeat of a small child, a child wrapped in swaddling clothes and set in a manger who later—at age 33—was wrapped in a linen cloth and set in a tomb. We offered him a cave to the inaccessible. St. Iranaeus maintained that he became human so that we might become more divine. If that is true, do we ever ponder that we have the potential of becoming divine? What would, what *does*, that mean?

But in this love story the romance exists in an entirely new register. As Benedict XVI points out in *Jesus of Nazareth, The Infancy Narratives*, "God is love. But love can also be hated when it challenges us to transcend ourselves. It is not a romantic 'good feeling.' We may consider redemptive love a force moving us toward 'wellness,' but it is not about basking in self-indulgence; on the contrary it is a liberation from imprisonment in self-absorption. This liberation comes at a price: the anguish of the cross. The prophecy of light and that of the Cross belong together."[1]

One day a Sister was trying to explain Jesus' birth and how much Jesus loved them to a group of small

---

[1] Benedict XVI, Pope. *Jesus of Nazareth: The Infancy Narratives.* Trans. Philip Whitmore, New York, NY; Image Books, 2012, p. 86.

children. She asked them "What was the mother of God's name?" All the hands shot up and they all said, "Mary." Then she asked what was her husband's name? Silence. No hands were raised. Finally, one child said, "Virg." Sister was startled at this and asked, "Why do you say that?" He replied, "Virg and Mary." Interestingly, this anecdote helps us to see that Jesus' willingness to pay the price was honed by his foster father, Joseph, who, though he made great sacrifices on his son's behalf, is often so obscure—in scripture and in the memory of Christians—that he clearly paid the price of giving without getting.

JESUS' BAPTISM

When Jesus was baptized by John the Baptist in the river Jordan, the heavens were opened and the Father said, "You are my beloved Son; with you I am well pleased" (Mk 1:11). Jesus received his strength by dwelling on this event as he entered the desert for forty days fasting, praying and being pricked by the devil—all of which toughened him up. Jesus began with the knowledge that he was loved by the Father as Isaiah assures us: "Because you are precious in my eyes and glorious, and because I love you" (43:4). Until we know that we are deeply loved by God we are just going through the motions. We, like Christ, need to pay the price of allowing it to become not just a head trip but a heart trip. Often my prayer mantra is, "Jesus my lover," but I still have a hard time believing he can love me because of all my sinfulness.

11

John the Baptist told people to repent, which they did at the river Jordan. Jesus went further and told them "Repent, and believe in the Gospel" (Mk 1:15). This is the price we need to pay, to not only change our minds, our attitudes, our way of living and turn toward God, but also to believe in the Good News, how much God loves us and how Jesus showed his love by dying on the cross. Too often we muddle through trying to grasp the unconditional love God has for us. If only we could set off alarm bells that would regularly remind us how God's love is everlasting. Then we might be less concerned about our mess of musts, "I must do this, must do that."

Jesus began his public ministry in the synagogue proclaiming the good news, "'The Spirit of the Lord is upon me because he has anointed me to bring glad tidings to the poor.' Rolling up the scroll he then stated, 'Today this scripture passage is fulfilled in your hearing'" (Lk 4:18, 21). These words are closely allied to his last words, "It is finished" (Jn 19:30). What is finished? What is fulfilled? God's will that Christ make his love incarnate for us. The price has been paid. But, again, we must pay the price, which is allowing our hearts to be altered by Christ, so we can become more Christlike.

IDENTITY CRISIS

Jesus asks the Apostles, "Who do the people say I am" (Mk 8:29)? One of the reasons the world is filled with so much poverty, crime, drugs, and obesity, one reason our social fabric is broken, is that we don't know who we are.

The simple "identity crisis" is the reason behind the
abundance of pain, suffering and grief, a grief that becomes
even more pronounced at the loss of a loved one or one's
job.

When someone asks you to recite your social
security number, your date of birth, your home address,
your e-mail, are you able to rattle them off without any
difficulty? But if we are asked our credit card number, how
many of us know it without looking it up? And yet for
how many of us this credit card number defines so much
of what we do, of what we've become! So many of our
transactions, like airline tickets, purchases in stores or
malls, are done through numbers. After a while we become
a number when dealing with banks, hospitals, government.
We can dehumanize ourselves by being more familiar with
our credit card numbers than the state of our souls.

Jesus treated individuals not as numbers, but as
people loved by God. A deaf and mute man is brought to
him who has no name. He doesn't say, "Ooh, the poor
fellow," or treat him as a statistic, someone to be ignored
and ridiculed. But the more he actually was a number the
less he could participate in society. He was unable to hear
or speak, and probably was ignored. Jesus sees in him a
person of infinite value, not a number or zero, and
therefore shows him caring attention. Jesus takes him away
from the crowd, recognizing and respecting his
individuality. We might call it a one-to-one miracle, as he
does more than lay hands on him as the people requested.
Then he puts his finger in the man's ears, an image that is

reminiscent of Michelangelo's Sistine's Chapel of God creating and giving life to Adam. But he does not stop there, taking spit and touching his tongue. We might be repulsed by this, but as John Shea points out, that spit symbolizes the Spirit connecting him with others. Jesus also says, "Ephphatha, be opened" (Mk 7:34). Now he is truly open to the Spirit, no longer a statistic, a nobody, an outcast. He also has been called to share the Spirit with others as he will be remembered as one Jesus encountered in the Decapolis.

Jesus also says to us "Ephphatha, be opened." We need to open our ears to hear his voice inviting us not to be frightened or reticent in reaching out to strangers. Can we respect them and not ignore or ridicule them? That can be costly. Isaiah instructs us, "This is the way, walk in it, when you turn to the right or to the left" (30:21). If we have heard and felt those words, Jesus will direct our paths to the right or left, but he will also assure us when we are unwilling to pay the price or are frightened, "Take courage, it is I; do not be afraid" (Mt. 14:27).

At Jesus' time associating with sinners, sick or unclean people like lepers, rendered a person unclean. That meant the person was unfit for community rituals like liturgy, common meals and even conversation. Jesus was aware of this and it also explains why the scribes and Pharisees were so upset because of his contact with outcasts. Can we imagine, as Barbara Brown asks us to do in *The Preaching Life,* Jesus at a plasma bank waiting to sell his blood, at a city jail talking to inmates on death row, speaking to a drug dealer at a meal, or putting his arm around someone with AIDS?

In *Jesus of Nazareth* Gerard Lohfink contends that everything Jesus did was meant to announce and proclaim God's reign. His parables and healings emphasized God's salvation making it present right now. The banquet imagery proclaimed God's abundance and the desire to share with others. In choosing the twelve Apostles, he wanted to symbolize his desire to gather all of Israel, indicating that salvation was extended to all. Is it any wonder then why he focused on Israel, where, in accordance with a long theological-cultural tradition, the family exercises loving service, hospitality, support of those in need and forgiveness through non-violence? A daunting challenge for all families, but Christ comes into each new bond established through the sacrament of marriage and asks the same.

ACTING ON JESUS' BELIEFS

Believing in Jesus is rather easy and harmless, but acting on his beliefs and carrying them out is indeed costly. Jesus did not allow his followers to take a cafeteria style approach to his teachings, wherein followers choose what they like or don't like. When he spoke about the kingdom, it was not about the future but about what was transpiring right *now*. This *now* continues in his followers. Some of the most basic costs include repentance, and the process of making his values our values, of making our values centered around our relationship with God and others. That can be counter-cultural, a precedent which was certainly set by the early Christians. They lived in a Roman culture of dominion by force, a military ethic that resulted in one of the most powerful armies in the world, an army that inflicted much excess violence. Jesus acted in the opposite way, teaching peace, showing love and accepting his own weakness.

As we read in the book of Hebrews, "Because he himself was tested through what he suffered, he is able to help those who are tested" (2:18). These are not empty words but are filled with consolation and potential to aid us in our suffering. The words can penetrate our soul and spirit, joints and marrow, and be a source of inspiration in our sufferings. We also read that "Son though he was he learned obedience from what he suffered and when he was made perfect, he became the source of eternal salvation" (5:8-9). Through the ordeals of life Jesus' humanity was made perfect through suffering. He had to learn to obey God in areas he never experienced before.

As Gary Wills states in *Why Priests, A Failed Tradition?*, "Jesus suffered the fate of other prophets. His own family thought him crazy (Mk 3:21). Men called him a bastard (Jn 8:4-1), unclean (Lk 11:38), a glutton (Lk 7:34), a devil (Jn 7:20). They tried to throw him off a cliff (Lk 4:29) or stone him (Jn 8:59)."[2]

As St. Anselm teaches us, "He paid the price," and the Father accepted. He struggled his whole life with

_____

[2] Wills, Gary. *Why Priests, A Failed Tradition?* New York, NY; Viking Penguin, 2013, p. 77.

the religious traditions of his time. He counteracted it with God's love and care for the outcasts and stretched the people's own boundaries. That is the true meaning of the cross. The true meaning of the cross is Jesus' willingness to die for us out of love. When Judas betrayed him for thirty pieces of silver, he called him friend. Jesus predicted that Peter would deny him not once but three times. And what does he say to Peter? Not a single word. Rather, he gives him a loving glance which melts his heart. That is what is needed in our society: more loving glances. Jesus turned the other cheek when confronted by his enemies and he invites us to do the same. Why didn't he fight back when he was falsely accused of blasphemy, of being a drunkard, an associate with sinners? Once he is seized by the soldiers in the garden, he offers no resistance and everything is done to him, all cruelty is lashed out at him. Why did he offer silent, nonviolent resistance to soldiers who mocked and spit on him? Why was he meek, offering the disciplined power of humility when opposition surrounded him? Was it because when he looked into the face of his enemies, the scribes and Pharisees, the chief priests, Pilate and the soldiers, he saw God? How could he strike out against the image of God when he came to redeem them? If we are disciples of Jesus we need to respond to opposition, rejection, hurts with non-violence. This word is often thrown around loosely, but embodying it is extremely costly.

In order to acquire anything we must pay a price —perhaps of money, perhaps, in the case of a gift, of gratitude. Anything worth having, costs something. Jesus said, "Enter through the narrow gate; for the gate is wide and the road broad that leads to destruction, and those who enter through it are many. How narrow the gate and constricted the road that leads to life. And those who find it are few" (Mt: 13-14). Are we willing to enter the narrow gate? Are we willing to pay the price?

If you want to capture the tensions and turmoil of Jesus' time, read Gerd Theissen's *The Shadow of the Galilean* which shows how Jesus affected his Jewish environment under Roman rule. Jesus was accused of being king of the Jews and hence a rival to Caesar, who was known as Caesar the Lord. The confrontation is also brought out by Edward Hays' *Pilate's Prisoner,* where Jesus is portrayed as a man of contradictions, a religious atheist who fails to address the Roman gods. He also has Jesus thinking to himself that he learned to endure harsh punishment from his father Joseph, which enabled him to endure the temptation in the garden and not to run away from the cross. Jesus was willing to pay the price of being a suffering servant and that is one of the reasons many did not accept him. They wanted a worldly Messiah who would overthrow the Roman empire. St. Paul states that Jesus is Lord risen from the dead and that is the good news. But what sort of Lord? Jesus fearlessly preached a different kingdom, one greater than the empire of Rome, an act which was considered high treason.

PASSION OF JESUS

Toward the end of a directed retreat I ask the retreatants to pray over one of the passion narratives. They are, however, encouraged to do this not as spectators but in a manner that helps them actually see how it pertains to their lives. Jesus was betrayed by Judas. Have they ever been betrayed by someone and how did they react? When Jesus went into the garden of Gethsemane to pray, St. Luke tells us "He was in such agony and he prayed so fervently that his sweat became like drops of blood falling to the ground" (22:44). Our response might be, "Oh, that is impossible." Many years ago a Doctor Barbet wrote a book entitled *Doctor at Calvary,* where he shows that it is possible for someone to suffer so intensely that the capillaries in our body actually break. That is probably what happened to Jesus. He prayed at a time of extreme sadness, thereby inviting us to pray when we are sad, troubled and vexed. As the Psalmist says, "On the day of distress I seek the Lord" (77:3). Jesus prayed while his Apostles slept and when he needed their support. There might be times when we feel the lack of support from others so we need to cry out, "Our help is in the name of the Lord" (Ps 124:8). We need to pray the way Jesus prayed when we request something from God, "Not my will but yours be done" (Lk 22:42), which can be very challenging and costly. He prayed to do the Father's will and paid the price of martyrdom. Jesus was strengthened in his agony by an angel as he was in the desert having fasted forty days. Similar help is given us in our suffering.

The scourging, as depicted in the movie *The Passion of Christ*, was most graphic and for some overdone. The innumerable lashes cut deeply into his flesh. Some slaves died from this torture. The fact that it was done in public added to the humiliation. But maybe the greatest humiliation was that, in accordance with Roman usage, he was stripped of all his clothing before being nailed to the cross. Jesus was also crowned with thorns, as the soldiers mocked, spat on him and hailed him as King of the Jews. In being crowned with thorns Christ's whole being was crowned with suffering. This was part of the "price" he paid. Jesus had fled earlier when they wanted to make him king. When our head suffers it affects our whole body. Just ask anyone suffering from migraine headaches. Pilate made attempts to release Jesus. Neither his eloquence nor his shrewd scheme to present them with a choice of Barabbas or Jesus prevailed. But he finally shifted the blame onto them when the people said, "his blood be upon us and our children" (Mt 27:25).

Ordinarily when the Roman sentence was pronounced there was a reprieve of some time. The chief priests, however, insisted that he be crucified immediately, and in fear the Roman state complied. The title of his guilt was put above his head on the cross: *King of the Jew*, it read. The procession moved through the most populous streets to allow others to look on and fear. It is difficult for us to imagine what Jesus suffered walking these hilly and uneven streets. His falling and rising many times under the weight of the cross remind us that when we fall we have to rise once more to assure us of eventual victory. Maybe his greatest grief was seeing his sorrowful mother. What a heart-rending scene that must have been when they met. They were not allowed to speak, but their looks spoke volumes. Mary looks at her son. All her moments of tenderness, protective care, and for this? She cannot save him. If she tries to stop the procession, she will be killed. And he will not be able to pay the price.

Jesus receives a cruel kind of sympathy when the soldiers prevail on Simon to help carry the cross. But even this forced pity is redeemed in time. It had such a profound effect on Simon and his family that two of his sons later became bishops. When the women heroically lament Jesus, he tells them not to weep for him but themselves and their children. Jesus constantly invites us to take up our cross, to pay with our own passions. How is it possible for someone who is suffering so much to turn outward to others? When we are in pain we have a tendency to turn in on ourselves. Veronica is rewarded for her heroism in offering Jesus her veil, in part because she overcame her own sorrow by prioritizing Christ's pain.

Once they reach Mount Calvary, Golgatha, or Skull's place—because it looked like a human skull—Jesus finally arrives at his destination. Executions were not allowed in the city walls, just as scapegoats laden with people's sins had to be led outside the camp. Having his hands nailed to the cross must have been most excruciating for Jesus. He was lifted up, as he said, that he might draw all to himself. The soldiers offered him wine mixed with myrrh, but Jesus refused it. Perhaps this is because he did not want to die in a stupor, like Socrates who was ordered to take hemlock. It is impossible to imagine the agony Jesus endured for three hours, and his ability to say, "Father forgive them, they know not what they do," and finally to utter "Father, into your hands I commend my spirit" (Lk 23: 34, 46).

On the surface Jesus was crucified because the Romans were convinced he was fostering a counterculture to Caesar. This meant he was a traitor. But he was willing to die for us that we might be willing to pay the price of acting as a counter culture in our society today. In *The Crucified Christ* Jurgen Moltmann maintains that non-Christians and atheists recognize the relevance or importance of Good Friday more readily than Christians because the senselessness of Christ's death offends and astonishes them. For us as Christians the cross is the ultimate expression of God's love for us, a love that refuses to lash out at others and their sinful ways. His ministry was consummated in crucifixion. Father Raniero Cantalamessa, a Capuchin and papal preacher, states that Jesus' death "has unmasked and broken forever the system that makes something sacral of violence."[3] Maybe Mary bowing her head in humility as she cradles the dead body of Jesus helps us to respond to, even if we cannot make sense of, the holocaust of Christ, and of the 20th Century's horrible Holocaust. It is the mystery of love confronting

---

[3] Winright, Tobias. "Gandolf, Gollum and the Death Penalty," *Sojourners.* Vol 42, No 1, January 2013, p.26.

the mystery of hate. We must embrace those shattered by evil, shattered by suffering. They cry out to like sirens in the night. Dorothy Day, quoting Dostoevsky, called it a "harsh and dreadful love" which challenged her to reach out to the poor and suffering.

THE RESURRECTION

The darkness of Good Friday gives way to the glorious resurrection of Jesus. What some considered a failure, including the disciples on the way to Emmaus, has turned into a triumph. The powerlessness of the cross leads to the power of the resurrection. "That is the rest of the story" as Paul Harvey would say. Jesus not only predicted his death but also that he would rise, and did it! He did the impossible. St. Augustine considered it a supreme and marvelous work. St. Paul provokes us by stating that if Christ has not risen then we might as well eat, drink and be merry because tomorrow we die and it is all over. An atheist one day asked a priest, "What if you die and find out that there is no future life?" The priest responded, "I am more concerned about you dying and finding out there is one."

Hope is one of the great fruits of Jesus' resurrection. St. Paul had to assure the Thessalonians that they needed hope. Many of them hoped that Jesus would come during their life time so they would not have to die. Paul assures us that hope will not disappoint. Hope links us to the past, bursts us into the present, and drives us into the future. Teihard de Chardin believed that a Christian cannot live except in and for the future. Karl Rahner maintained that hope is an abandonment to an unfathomable God. Robert Barron calls hope a non-negotiable.

In his encyclical on hope Benedict XVI states that those who hope live a different and new life. They remain grounded. Hope-filled people are not easily discouraged when faced with their darkest hours, trials and difficulties. Winston Churchill claimed he was an optimist because there was not much room for anything else. But Christians have something so much more than blind optimism. They have a concrete hope rooted in faith in the historical and transcending reality of Christ. St. Paul grew inwardly as he paid the price outwardly. He wrote, "We are not discouraged, rather, although our outer self is wasting away, our inner self is being renewed day by day" (2 Cor 4:16). Hope-filled people never give up. Toward the end of his life Beethoven life became deaf, but he wrote some of his beautiful music when he could hear nothing. Toward the end of his life Milton became blind, but he wrote some of his most beautiful poetry when he was blind. It took Brahms twenty years before he finally finished his first symphony. Look how long Thomas Edison toiled before he finally discovered the electric light bulb. Someone asked him, "Did you not look upon those experiments as useless?" He answered, "No, they proved to me what would not work."

Some people, however, have no hope. They may be former optimists who hoped not in God but in something others promised, or in a too-grand vision of themselves. They may find life meaningless, useless and ready to commit suicide. I remember visiting a man in the hospital who said, "I almost did it" when I entered the room. "Did what," I asked? "I almost committed suicide." Then he told me his story. All of us have a story to tell, but the problem is that there are not enough listeners. He told me how he lost his job, his wife divorced him, the children will not have anything to do with him. Then he showed me a tiny crucifix. "Do you notice anything about it," he asked. I answered, "Yes, the corpus is partially broken off." He told me that when he was ready to commit suicide, he grasped the crucifix so hard that he broke it. "But, that," he said, "saved my life."

Dorothy Day came in contact with similar people and inspired much hope in them. She insisted that too much problem analysis leads to paralysis. Day wanted action because there was much to be done. That action is being embodied anew in the topmost tier of the Church. Pope Francis washed the feet of 12 young inmates at a juvenile detention facility near Rome and told them, "Don't lose hope. With hope you can always go on." Jesus' suffering, death and resurrection spur us on to deepen our commitment in carrying on his ministry to others as his disciples in hope.

SCRIPTURE PASSAGES FOR REFLECTION

"The word became flesh and made his dwelling among us."
(Jn 1:14)

"You are my beloved son, with you I am well pleased."
(Mk 1:11)

"Repent and believe in the Gospel."
(Mk 1:15)

"Take courage it is I; do not be afraid."
(Mt 14:27)

"Because he himself was tested through what he suffered he is able to help those who are tested."
(Heb 2:18)

QUESTIONS TO CONSIDER

1. How does the mystery of the Incarnation touch or influence your life?
2. Do you feel deeply how much you are loved by God, and how has it changed your life?
3. Where do you need to repent or convert?
4. What aspect of the passion do you find most challenging?
5. How do you react to insult, rejection, and not being loved?

CHAPTER TWO
HOW COSTLY IS DISCIPLESHIP?

If we are to carry on the ministry of Jesus, we have to embrace discipleship. The word disciple means "a learner, one who has not yet arrived, on the way to conversion." The word is used at least two hundred and fifty times in the Gospels. It is a call from God with a cost. When we do not know the price of an object or need a roof or basement repaired, we often ask, "How much will it cost?" This is especially true when companies or contractors have to bid on certain projects. Then we have to make a decision. Are we willing to pay the price or the cost? When we approach Christianity we countenance something infinitely more costly than the items of a game show such as "The Price is Right." Because of our conventional understanding of cost/benefit, we often respond that Christianity costs too much. But what a price some people will pay to climb the ladder of success! Jesus used the parable of a man who wanted to build a tower, but had to first sit down and calculate the cost: was there enough money for its completion? If he starts a building and is unable to finish he will be laughed at and ridiculed.

Discipleship means getting to know Jesus. We get to know others gradually by spending time with them. The Apostles had a high esteem of Jesus because of his many miracles of mercy. But their knowledge of Jesus was rather superficial, a phenomenon that is brought out most graphically by Peter, who eventually denied him. We might possess a lot of factual knowledge about Jesus but still not really know him. If we are to be his disciples, we have to move from a superficial relationship to an intimate, personal one. Once we know people on an intimate level, we can become committed to them. Before the Apostles came to possess a truly intimate bond with Christ, they needed to undergo an extensive process of formation and purgation, but once the Spirit descended on them in tongues of fire, that changed their lives dramatically. The same can be true of us. St. Paul maintained that "No one can say that Jesus is Lord, except by the Holy Spirit" (I Cor 12:3). We therefore also need to be fully open to the Holy Spirit who can assist us in this process.

We might envision discipleship as existing in stages. First is God's call. Each of our "calls" comes in a similar manner. Unlike Saul, Israel's first king, Elisha is called while plowing his fields. His possession of twelve oxen might indicate that he was well off or that he had joined a communal agricultural effort. We cannot help noticing that in spite of the fact he was settled or well off he had no second thoughts but was willing to follow Elijah. He did, however, want to bid farewell to both of his parents, which is understandable in light of his close kinship or relationship to his family. The case is also true of anyone who, engaged in a close relationship, wishes to tie up loose ends before they embark more fully on the way of God. The same tension arises when someone feels called to the priesthood, religious life, deaconate, or any other church ministry that involves a cost. Elijah does not grant the request and, at first blush, it sounds a bit harsh. But isn't Jesus' response to his disciples' similar requests even harsher: "Let the dead bury the dead" (Lk 9:60)? What are the implications for Elisha? Now he is commissioned to be a prophet and is challenged to make a radical break with the past. His final response, his "yes," is praiseworthy because he is willing to pay the price of slaughtering the oxen and using the plowing equipment for firewood. All of this indicates a severance with the past. Now he is totally committed to his ministry which is brought out thoroughly by his feeding the people.

In Greek the word for "church" is *ekklesia, ek* meaning out, and *kaleo* meaning call. If we wish to be part of the Church we need to be sensitive to the voice that calls. The Popes and Bishops have highlighted this often. New names were given to Abram, Jacob, Saul and Peter. But Moses clung to the old ways of acting until late in life. He had a vicious temper, but later we read that he became the "meekest man on the face of the earth" (Num 12:3). Walter Brueggemann believes we have been called into an everlasting relationship with God. The call is ongoing, much like ongoing conversion. We might be called to live a simpler life style, to reach out to the sick and dying, to protest against social injustice, to work with HIV and AIDS patients. James Dunn maintains "There is a disturbing quality about the urgency of Jesus' call, a shaking of the foundations which those who want a quiet life are bound to resent and resist."[4] We are not necessarily called, however, to be another St. Francis of Assisi, Mother Teresa, or Dorothy Day, but God asks us *all* to become detached from material things and possessions. When true disciples enter a city, the power structure is disturbed. Things change. They obey God rather than others. If we are to embody discipleship we need to recapture the courage, bravery and sacrificial spirit of the early church. Sometimes the call comes from inside of us, rather than from without. As Ilia Delio points out in *The Emerging Christ* "In the early days of Christianity, prior to the age of Constantine, to be a Christian meant accepting costly discipleship."[5] While Jesus was traveling, a man came to him saying "I will follow you wherever you go" (Lk 9:57). His application sounds like that of an ideal recruit. But Jesus reminds him that if he wants to fulfill his ambitious goal he needs to have his eyes wide open—not dazzled by unrealistic idealism. Enthusiasm can be very transitory and fickle, as is evident from the story of the rich young man. We can burst forth in a flourish only to falter along the way because of the sacrifices demanded of us. Jesus doesn't always look for those who can do the job. Rather, he surprises us by calling those who feel they cannot. "Competent" individuals often proceed on their own steam, whereas those who feel inadequate usually conquer

4 Dunn, James. *Jesus' Call to Discipleship.* New York, NY; Cambridge University Press, 1992, p. 16.

5 Delio, Ilia. *The Emerging Christ.* Maryknoll, New York; Orbis Press, 2016, p. 59.

life's trials by abandonment to divine providence, or a total reliance on God. Grace can seep through the cracks of our inabilities, while self sufficiency often blocks it. Life in Christ calls us to unfeigned integrity. Jesus clearly stated, "I came so that they might have life and have it abundantly" (Jn 10:10). In other words, discipleship means expansion, not constriction; freedom, not bondage; robust joyfulness, not gloomy pietism. We do not limp between two options. Some of the most difficult choices are not between good and evil, but rather between good and excellent or good and beatitude. We cannot retrieve into our protective shells claiming that nothing can be done. The chase is on.

The second stage of discipleship involves disturbance or displacement. Jesus gave up heaven to be with us. Again as St. Paul wrote, "He emptied himself, taking the form of a slave, coming in human likeness, and found human in appearance, he humbled himself, becoming obedient to death, even death on a cross" (Phil 2: 7-8). A greater displacement cannot be conceived. Displacement suggests a move or shift from the ordinary. Jesus said, "If anyone comes to me without hating his father and mother, wife and children, brothers and sisters, and even his own life, he cannot be my disciple" (Lk 14:26). It is a call away from having things under control, away from a scenario in which we feel very comfortable in our warm cocoon. In nearly every culture much pressure exists to stay with the ordinary and the comforts of convention.

Jesus made it very clear that the conditions for discipleship are very challenging, "If anyone wishes to come after me, he must deny himself and take up his cross daily and follow me. For whoever wishes to save his life will lose it, but whoever loses his life for my sake will save it" (Lk 9:23). In Daniel Berrigan's words, we have to look good on wood. The Apostles were called to leave the security of their boats, nets and families and put out into deeper waters to follow Jesus. A true disciple has to become detached from one's career, projects, plans, pleasure, the "need" to be first, and even from one's will. Edwina Gately spoke of this as comparable to living on the prophetic edge. The danger always exists: by our very nature we want to play it safe rather than be sharp and alert living on the precipice. Someone said to Jesus, "I will follow you, Lord, but first let me say farewell to my family at home." Jesus said to him, "No one sets a hand to the plow and looks to what was left behind is fit for the kingdom of God" (Lk 9: 23-24, 61-62). If we are to become Jesus' disciple we must do so without compromise, freed from any kind of distraction. Breaking ties can be very painful because the tug of the old will always be there, but are we willing to pay the price of putting our hand to the plow and not looking back? Yes it hurts, but yes it leads to freedom.

Mary is the first and perfect disciple because she hears God's word, accepts it and gives her "yes." A true disciple is someone who is both open to hearing God's word and willing to carry it out in one's life. Mary makes discipleship a lived reality. She did not know, however, where this discipleship would lead her. No script was given her concerning Bethlehem, Egypt, the loss of the child in the temple, Nazareth, Cana and especially Calvary. Mary knew what it was like to be a displaced person or a refugee in a foreign land. She felt the pain of loss of her child in the temple, able therefore to identify with parents who feel the loss of their child to drugs, gangs or the life of a runaway. Her widowhood undoubtedly brought many tears, as did the experience of holding Jesus in her arms after he had been taken down from the cross. Discipleship demands complete and wholehearted commitment to Jesus regardless of our state in life, family ties, or occupation. Commitment, however, does not empty life of meaning. Yes, all other concerns have to be put on the back burner or left behind, but we find new meaning in a way we never knew before. Can we be true Christians today without making a total commitment to Christ? Any good team wants commitment of all of its players or members. Total commitment brings success. We encounter many "followers of Jesus" today but how many committed disciples? Dietrich Bonhoeffer stated that when Christ calls, he bids us come and die. When his friends made an attempt to liberate him from prison, Bonhoeffer decided to remain there, and later he was hanged. Discipleship means to identify ourselves publicly with Christ as Lord in our lives despite the cost. To acknowledge him as Lord means that we see him as more important than, as Lord of, our material possessions. It also means that we are willing to speak out against any injustice. The price of silence is betrayal.

TRUE DISCIPLES

In 1514, at the age of thirty, Bartolome de las Casas gave up his lands and the Indians he possessed and joined the Dominicans. Having witnessed the atrocities and cruelties done to the poor, atrocities before which he did at first remain silent, he later became their passionate and prophetic defender through his preaching. He went so far as to refuse absolution to any Spaniard who would not free his Indian slaves. This resulted in death threats from the Spanish court. But las Casas remained faithful in defending their dignity and their religious liberty, thereby challenging the legality of the Spanish conquests.

Think of all the people in the world today who have been displaced by war and violence. I read recently that there are some 134 million migrants who fit into this category. Our salvation history is replete with refugees and migrants. Abram was called from his familiar land out into an unknown place, by a God he hardly knew. He was a believer in many gods. Yet, he was willing to follow God not knowing what lay in store for him. Mary wanted to remain a virgin but was given the gift of both motherhood *and* virginity. Because of his traumatic encounter with Jesus, Saul took another road than Damascus and he became the apostle to the Gentiles. But the rich young man was unable to accept Jesus' challenge to sell all that he had and follow him (Lk 18:18-23). This is one of the saddest stories in the Gospel. I remember when, having just joined the Capuchins, I gave the money saved in the bank to my parents. It was a very challenging experience for me because I worked hard to earn the money. I earned fifty cents a week helping a man who owned a tavern, cleaning spittoons, sweeping floors and replenishing soda. It is difficult to let go of our possessions or things that we have accumulated. Often I encourage people to have garage sales or to give away what they are not using to Good Will, or the Capuchins, the latter of which produces a laugh. You will not find a U-haul behind a hearse. As one pastor use to say, "You cannot take it with you, but you can always send it ahead." C.S. Lewis gave his book royalties to charity and lived on a very modest income as a University professor. To be a disciple of Jesus we have to cast out into the deeper waters and not hug the safe shoreline. Edwina Gately could have stayed home in the peace and safety of Lancaster, England. Instead she stepped out of her comfort zone and founded a lay Volunteer Missionary Movement in Uganda, East Africa, in 1969. Now those who have followed in her footsteps are located in more than 40 countries.

Discipleship is not always landlocked. Todd Love is a triple amputee who lost both of his legs and an arm as a Marine in Afghanistan. His father carries him to a river where he is placed in a kayak by a trained instructor. Love's whole world changes because he feels free and it is the best therapy for him. The kayaking is made possible through the efforts of Joe Morini who has reached out to disabled veterans. He felt the need to be sent out, like the disciples, to help others.

The story of sister Dorothy Stang, a Notre Dame sister, is told in *The Greatest Gift*. She worked among the poorest in Brazil and incurred the wrath of people who were using the poor for their own ends. When she came back to the states for a visit, many told her not to return because there was a price on her head. But she insisted that these were her people and wanted to go back to help the poorest of the poor in their struggle. Sister Dorothy did not offer a paltry palette of words, but backed them up with her solid convictions. She was brutally murdered, but she fulfilled her dream of Christ's maxim that no one has greater love than to lay down one's life for one's friends.

The paradox of being displaced or separated is that people in this condition often find themselves in deeper union with others, *in* the world but not *of* the world. Thomas Merton felt that even in his Trappist monastery he could be everywhere. Dietrich Bonhoeffer left the United States for Germany—where he strongly resisted Hitler's euthanasia programs and genocide against the Jews. He also was involved in plans to assassinate Hitler, for which he was imprisoned by the Nazis and later hanged in April 1945, twenty-three days before the Nazis surrendered. He felt closely allied with the clergy as well as the broader church and the people, whom he was not afraid to confront. Dorothy Day went to Bowery to become more intimately united with the poor. Mother Teresa left her own community to start her own, ministering also to the poorest of the poor whom she loved very much. St. Francis of Assisi stripped himself of all his clothes so that he could identify more radically with the poor. Displacements lead to deeper union with others. St. Paul experienced this with the Corinthians when he wrote, "I will most gladly spend and be utterly spent for your sakes" (2 Cor 12:15).

If these displacements are difficult, inner ones are even more challenging. We might have to change the way we think or act. Most of us are in need of conversion away from resentment, anger, bitterness, grudges or apathy. We need to reach out to the sick and dying, protesting against some social injustice by marching in a non-violent way, working with HIV or AIDS people which can stretch our discipleship to the limit.

In *Waiting for God* Simone Weil, a French philosopher and mystic, maintains that spiritual change or transformation can take place only when we are willing to let go of our position as the center of things. Falling into this trap is falling for a "false divinity" or a form of idolatry. Denying oneself as center is integral to true discipleship and is costly. Often we are unable or unwilling to detect it and therefore don't eradicate our vanity or pride. Jesus perceived this in people he encountered as well as in the Apostles. To be true disciples means to be drawn out of ourselves by Jesus rather than to remain centered on ourselves. We need to center our lives on Jesus who knows and cares for us, and not on ourselves—in part because we do not know ourselves, and so we cannot and faithfully and truthfully be our own light as he can. This will enable us to face all our struggles, hardships and trials. Then, like the disciples on the way to Emmaus, our eyes will be opened because we have centered our lives on Jesus and will be more ready to be sent out.

BEING SENT OUT

The third stage of discipleship, then, is being sent out. We are co-missioned rather than commissioned. This is one of the main purposes of discipleship. Jesus sent out his seventy-two disciples stating that "The harvest is abundant but the laborers are few; so ask the master of the harvest to send out laborers for his harvest" (Lk 10:2). We are to proclaim the Good News to others, for Jesus assures us that, "Whoever listens to you listens to me" (Lk 10:16). Even the possessed man whom Jesus cured wanted to go with him, but Jesus said, "Go home to your family and announce to them all that the Lord in his pity has done for you" (Mk 5:19). All of us are gifted, and Jesus reminds us that, ""Without cost you have received; without cost you are to give" (Mt 10:8). The cost might entail not clinging to material things or persons. It also means not unduly clinging to Jesus, at least when our clinging to him prevents us from acts of love. Ilia Delio states in *The Emerging Christ* "To be a disciple of Jesus is not to cling to Jesus (like Mary Magdalene) but to go forth as part of the cosmic family, to enter into new relationships."[6] Being

---

[6] Delio. *The Emerging Christ*, p. 110.

a disciple means doing both—cling at times, and at other times letting go.

Many individuals experience a rapture which opens them to a mission. Moses had it with the burning bush. Isaiah had a glorious view of cascading angels and a heavenly throne which ended with, "Whom shall I send" (6:8)? On his way to Damascus, Saul was struck blind, which turned his life upside down. Peter, James and John were given a glimpse of Jesus' divinity at the transfiguration. These and many more incidents indicate how "God, it seems, refuses to disclose himself without a 'price,' without the ulterior motive of commissioning the visionary for service to the whole community."[7] But they had to struggle in carrying out their missions.

Discipleship demands struggle with self control. We don't realize how much we want to control our own lives, the lives of others, and even God. We want our own way. In contrast Jesus made it clear how he came to do God's will not his own. Too often our lives revolve around a lot of I's and we might even border on being narcissistic. This was the problem that the Scribes and Pharisees had and we know how Jesus treated them with his many woes.

We struggle with self gratification. When we are hungry we eat; when lazy we sleep or idle away our time especially watching television and becoming couch potatoes. We often do not realize how much we seek our comfort zones and refuse to radically commit ourselves to a

---

7 Barron, Robert. *And Now I See. . .* New York, NY; Crossroad,1998, p.73.

passionate love of God and others. To be a disciple of Jesus we need to be more marathon runners than sprinters. Even in preparing our meals we prefer the microwave rather than the crock pot.

Good examples are people who are willing to spend time in Appalachia working with the poor. I know of a doctor and a deacon who volunteer their services to minister in Guatemala. These are ordinary people "being sent out." Discipleship requires a generous heart. Like the psalmist we take refuge and cling to God, even as we pour ourselves out for others. We have the assurance that God makes our destiny secure and we will not be shaken. David O'Brien, a University professor at Dayton, Ohio, writes that "the test of Christian discipleship is the life we live."[8] Discipleship is not meant for the few but for all. James Dobson, the founder of Focus on the Family, believes that our society is facing a severe crisis in which our moral decline threatens our very existence. At seventy-three plus he has joined a daily radio program that has 1.5 million listeners a day on one thousand stations, and he advocates for social change.

We might not be able to accomplish what he does. But discipleship puts us directly in the center of the arena where we make hard choices between love and hatred, despair and hope, nursed hurts and genuine forgiveness, indifference and caring, violence and peace. Sometimes our decision can result in family members getting upset and

---

8 O'Brien, David. "Change the Church," *America.* Vol. 207, No. 4, Aug 13, p. 25.

even disowning us. Recall Fathima Rifqa Bary, a Muslim, whose father threatened to kill her if she converted to Christianity. These happenings and others amaze and often baffle us. And yet, we must be ready to sacrifice the same. Even more so, the wounds and scars inflicted on us cannot compare to what Jesus endured on the cross where he willingly paid the price of his blood. According to Father Larry Richards who wrote *Be a Man!* a disciple "is a person who is willing to die to himself and enter into a relationship with Jesus."[9] Our identity as disciples of Jesus is found in our acceptance of suffering, death and resurrection.

Clashes with discipleship will arise because of family obligation, raising children, taking care of elderly parents, and the need to earn a living. Conflicts are bound to arise and are impossible to avoid because necessary crosses cause many of them. But we can negotiate or integrate them into our lives on our pilgrim journey. Jesus invites us to take up our cross each day and follow in his footsteps. These daily dyings enlighten us to our true self, not the false self who resists the self-emptying of our attachments.

Our central attachment has to be God. All others are secondary. We naturally feel attracted to some people, but that feeling should be stronger in our relationship with God. Is this true in our lives? By detaching ourselves from persons and things we can more easily be drawn toward

9 Richards, Larry. *Be A Man!* San Francisco, CA. Ignatius Press, 2009, p. 58.

our primary attachment to God. Then we can more readily realize what the psalmist expressed, "The Lord is my shepherd, there is nothing I shall want" (Ps 23). In order to express these tender and affective thoughts the psalmist had to be filled with God. No wonder the saints were able to cling to God—because nothing else could satisfy them. Christ and St. Paul encourage us to love, to show the highest kind of love, which Pope Emeritus Benedict XVI writes about in his beautiful encyclical on love, a total and complete commitment, not a half-hearted response. Loving the way Jesus did leads to a new kind of freedom, a freedom that enables us to accept and live the cost of discipleship, to be sent out amidst even those we find hardest to love. According to Scripture scholar Donald Senior, love of enemies is one of the most characteristic teachings of Jesus. We love those who hate us because God loves them. As disciples we are made new; we are built, or wired, for love, forgiveness and compassion. But we need to examine our motivation. Seneca tells the story of Nero who kills a man's son and then invites the father to a dinner. The man does not want to retaliate because he was afraid he will kill his other son. He was afraid of something worse could happen. Seneca also tells the story of a man who was being nipped by a small dog and yet refused to kick him to show his superiority over the dog.

When Jesus asked James and John, "What do you wish (me) to do for you?" They answered him, "Grant that in your glory we may sit one at your right and the other at your left." Jesus said to them, "You do not know what you are asking" (Mk 10:36-38). Jesus had another lesson for them and us to learn about discipleship. Just because the cost is high, we cannot count on "rewards." Jesus wanted them to learn more about servant leadership and so he said, "Whoever wishes to be first among will be the slave of all. For the son of man did not come to be served but serve and give his life as a ransom for many" (Mk 10:44-45). We need to pray that we might be able to put aside our hope for glory and honor in our lives. We need courage to reach out to the lost and forgotten, removing any obstacles that block our vision for true discipleship. The cost of discipleship is brought out most forcefully in the life of Bonhoeffer who insists that there is no cheap grace. The price tag is high because once we embrace what it means, dominant "society" might consider us foolish and silly. Will we take the road less traveled in spite of the fact that there might be more bumps, pot holes, curves, twists and turns? Jesus made it clear when he said,"Many are invited, but few are chosen" (Mt 22:14). He also challenged us "Unless your righteousness surpasses that of the scribes and Pharisees, you will not enter into the kingdom of heaven" (Mt 5:20).

Jesus spelled out what it means to be his disciple when he said, "Do not think that I have come to bring peace upon the earth. I have come to bring not peace but the sword. For I have come to set a man against his father, a daughter against her mother, and a daughter-in-law against her mother-in-law; and one's enemies will be those of his household" (Mt. 10:34-36). Jesus' honesty is certainly on display; he laid it on the line. No pussyfooting!

The demands of discipleship will entail warfare and our foes might be in our own household. While enumerating his suffering, St. Paul wrote about false brothers. The Jews understood the Day of the Lord as meaning a division in families, a splitting up of homes. We can get some taste of this division when we consider the misunderstanding and tension that results when an adherent of Islam converts to Christianity. One spouse might be a Democrat and the other a Republican. We must be willing to endure the tension of discipleship. Great causes will divide people. How much more will Christ?

DISCIPLINE AND DISCIPLESHIP

When we hear the word "discipline" we often react negatively because it connotes doing something that we don't like to do. We might be willing to take out the garbage or feed the dog rather than taking on something more challenging. Indeed, discipline is a word many are not terribly fond of. Proverbs is rather explicit on the matter, "He will die from lack of discipline" (5:23). How many of us discipline ourselves spiritually as we do physically? How disciplined are we in what we eat or drink, in what we see on TV? One Archbishop agreed that seventy percent of the problems he deals with concern themselves with lust, which so often originates from a lack of discipline over our eyes—and our hearts. Job made a covenant with his eyes through which he determined not to look lustfully on a woman (31:1). As Capuchin novices we were taught the importance of custody of the eyes, not realizing at that time how important it was. We are what we look at. This is so true regarding pornography— sexuality beyond all bounds of discipline—which is becoming an epidemic in our society. I take time with many individuals who confess this in the sacrament of reconciliation.

Discipline without discipleship can lead to drudgery due to our own lack of vision. Proverbs tells us that where there is no vision, people will certainly perish. Jesus' discipline is not a drudgery or something imposed by others—not even by God—but is self imposed. Paul encouraged Timothy to discipline himself (I Tim 4:7-8). Actually, discipline is derived from "discipleship" which means "to dedicate oneself to a person or a cause." Jesus was very disciplined, as manifested by his resolution to go up to Jerusalem to suffer, die and rise. Nothing could deter him from this resolution or mission. Everything he did was oriented to this goal. How resolute or disciplined are we? Can nothing deter us from our goal? St. Paul articulates the posture of one who is disciplined when he writes, "Forgetting what lies behind but straining forward to what lies ahead. I continue my pursuit toward the goal, the prize of God's upward calling, in Christ Jesus" (Phil 3:13-14). Paul certainly fulfilled what Joseph Conrad believed necessary that "there is no rest for the messenger until the message has been delivered."[10] St. Paul certainly understood

---

[10] Richards, Larry. *Be A Man!* San Francisco, CA; Ignatius Press, 2009, p. 58.

the cost of discipleship, considering everything as rubbish that he might gain Christ (Phil. 3:8). In *To Be a Man* Father Larry insists that discipline will cost you greatly. So often we are willing to pay high prices for quality food, cars, or entertainment. Yet, how often are we willing to pay with our very being? True discipleship leads us to the cross, and how many of us are willing to follow Jesus there?

Discipline is the hard edge of discipleship because it means delayed satisfaction. When we lack discipline in the market place, we experience economic thrombosis. What about a spiritual thrombosis, which can result in a toxic backwash? Henri Nouwen believed that discipline without discipleship is comparable to running a marathon without practicing, or to practicing but never running in the true race. And yet, he maintained that spiritual discipline is not the same as found in sports. In *Zen in the Art of Archery* Eugene Engel shows that the years of practice undertaken by Japanese archer enabled him to develop a spiritual discipline. Spiritual discipline requires that we create the space in which we are open to the Spirit and are ready and able to respond freely to the Spirit's promptings. A skilled musician can play a piece of music effortlessly, but it undoubtedly took many years of disciplined practice. As a boy, the famous cellist Pablo Casals did little else but practice the Bach cello suites from a worn copy his mother had given him. A prominent composer heard him and Casals was invited to play before a prominent royal Spanish family. His fame skyrocketed and he was invited to perform before Queen Victoria and, at 85 years of age, before President John F. Kennedy. Even at the age of ninety-three Casals practiced three hours daily. When asked why, he responded that he experienced some improvement. He believed that in retiring we die. Just so, if we ever cease to practice our imitation of Christ, we die.

Eugen Herrigel, a German philosopher, argues that to become a true disciple of Jesus we need superior qualities like love, meekness, mercy, purity of heart and peacemaking. And yet, true character is not built in a single act but over a lifetime of discipline. All of us are invited by Jesus to be more than a *follower*. But becoming his what he calls us to be—his disciples—is, as we have seen, challenging. As we embark more fully on this way we must gain a greater understanding of how dangerous, costly it is to be a Christian.

SCRIPTURAL PASSAGES FOR REFLECTION

"No one can say that Jesus is Lord, except by the Holy Spirit."

(I Cor 12:3)

"I will follow you wherever you go."

(Lk 9:57)

"I came that you might have life and have it abundantly."

(Jn 10:10)

"For whoever wishes to save his life will lose it, but whoever loses his life for my sake will save it."

(Lk 9:23)

"I will most gladly spend and be utterly spent for yourselves."

(2 Cor 12:15)

QUESTIONS TO CONSIDER

1. How do you deepen your call to discipleship? What are the obstacles?
2. How can you live on the "prophetic edge" as Edwina Gately suggests?
3. What inner displacements like anger, resentment, hurts, do you find most challenging?
4. How can you prevent yourself from clinging to material things, or the trap of consumerism?
5. How can you show the highest kind of love? What discipline is necessary?

CHAPTER THREE
BEING A CHRISTIAN: DANGEROUS AND COSTLY

Father Rutilio Grande, who was killed in El Salvador in 1977, who spent his life with the poor, said quite openly that it's dangerous to be Christian in the world today. Anti-Christian violence is extensive and it is difficult to know the exact number of people who suffer persecution. The threats often shed more heat than light. Todd Johnson of the World Christian Encyclopedia and Word Christian Database, estimates there are 70 million martyrs since the time of Christ, half of whom perished in the 20th century, most as a result of the Nazis and Soviets. If we average that out, it means eleven Christians are killed every hour each day. Father Gianni Criveller, a professor at the Holy Spirit seminary in Hong Kong, states that China has changed much but a persecutive religious policy has continued. Cardinal Kurt Koch, an official Vatican leader of ecumenism, believes an "ecumenism of the martyrs" will be the future push for Christian unity. John Allen Jr. a journalist, who occasionally writes about Christian persecution, maintains that the United States should play a more active role addressing the global war on Christians by using all the media traction possible.

Are we ready to pay the price of martyrdom—or at least the price of those little martyrdoms of daily sacrifice—in Christ's name? The poor widow in the Gospel was willing; she gave her two tiny coins, which were half the size of a penny. The little money really cost her, whereas the others gave of their surplus. We often give from our surplus as well. Protestants and Evangelicals give more generously than Catholics; this has been documented. Human beings have a proclivity to give as long as our comfort zones are not threatened. Theologian Langdon Gilkey has written a narrative *Shantung Compound*, a narrative about life in a Japanese internment camp during World War II. According to Gilkey, the prisoners were treated rather well, but once conflicts arose and people were asked to concede their comfort zones for the common good, they changed rather quickly, and were not willing to compromise. They complained rather vocally and were very resentful over the idea of making small sacrifices. This convinced Gilkey that most human beings are deeply narcissistic. For Gilkey, we are generous as long as it doesn't cost us or infringe on our comfort zones. Can we work against this tendency?

Someone might ask us, "Do you have any plans for Saturday?" and then ask if we are willing to do the person a favor. But we often want to know what is involved, how long it might take, *before* we make the commitment. We want to know what it will cost us before we agree. We tell ourselves, and make clear to the person asking us, that more information is needed. When Jesus invites us to, "Come, follow me," what is our response, what objections do we offer? Is there enough fire beneath the smoke of our desire? As Tim Allen said, we can drift through life sideways.

What distinguishes martyrs is their willingness to pay the *price of their lives* through their dedication and witness to justice and reconciliation. We know this influenced the growth of the early Church. In 2000, Pope John Paul II established a commission to study Christian martyrs of the 20th century. The fervor around the project died down, but it has gained momentum again through the efforts of writers such as John Allen Jr. On September 12, 2012, the U.S. Catholic Bishops held a religious freedom conference in Washington D.C. Here they addressed this complicated problem of how we maintain our freedom under trying circumstances. How has the Church carried out this challenge? How can we enliven our willingness to sacrifice ourselves for the life of the Church? Pope Emeritus Benedict XVI has made a connection between the Eucharist and the martyrs. Ignatius of Antioch believed martyrdom is a Eucharistic act. By partaking of Christ's self-gift, we ourselves can become more and more self-gift. The Church proclaims the fact that martyrs are not just those who die as victims of hatred directed toward their faith, but also those whose deaths are acts of justice which were motivated by those victims. During WWII, Father Kolbe was arrested because he was a Franciscan priest, but he considered his death as more just than that of the man whose place he took, a family man who lived for many years beyond this moment of sacrifice.

Martyrdom is powerfully portrayed in the life of Christian de Cherge who was abbot of a Trappist monastery in Atlas, Algeria. The film *Of God's and Men* showed these monks befriending so many people, including Muslims, through their medical practices. When civil war broke out, they were given a choice to stay and be killed or leave. They stayed. In a letter he composed soon before his death, Abbot de Cherge made it clear that he forgave his murderers.[11]

All of us who are Christians, Jews, or Muslims, have Abraham as our father in faith, so when any religious group is attacked or insulted, we who claim to be children of Abraham need to respond in solidarity. As Pope John Paul II pointed out, it is possible to be united to others despite our differences. He urged us to pursue deeper union with the Muslims through dialogue and a faith-based relationship. Muslims suffer the same atrocities as Christians; their mosques and Islamic centers are desecrated and burned. In New York, billboards advertize all Mulsims as savages, thereby distorting their religious beliefs. We need to support them, and teachers—in the home and classrooms—have an obligation to instruct their students that hatred of any religious group is unethical and is a form of racism. It is sacrilegious to burn a Qur'an or make a hate-filled video about Muslims. Pope Emeritus Benedict XVI has insisted that we respect their religious symbols.

---

[11] Philpott, Daniel. "Modern Martyrs," *America.* Vol. 207, No 14, 2012, pp. 13-18.

In a roundabout way—and I here do not at all wish to condone their actions—suicide bombers beg us to answer the question, *What will I die for?* This is a very important question. We might respond that we will die for this but not for that. Maybe we need to die before we die, so that when we die we are already dead to the world, dead to ourselves. Paul, ever the holy provoker, asks us, "Do you not know that we who were baptized into Christ Jesus were baptized into his death (Rom 6:3)? Too often we are looking for a cushion to soften our fall. We have deserts of fears, oceans of doubts and mountains of sacrifices that seem overwhelming. Old habits have a tendency to assert their grip and often the possibility of overcoming them appears to be too costly. Yet we must not let the call to martyrdom, direct or quiet and daily, be smothered by lesser things.

RELIGIOUS FREEDOM

At the end of World War II, Edwin O'Hara and the courageous Maryknoll Sisters made a decision to hire and train black physicians while accepting black patients at Queen of Heaven Hospital in Kansas City. They opposed segregated hospitals despite the fact that the local (unlike the federal) government said "No," and were ready to close them down. O'Hara and the sisters dared the government, and the members of Maryknoll prevailed because of their willingness to pay the price of opposition. Don't we face a similar obligation when the government tries to force us to do something against what we believe? We also need to take a strong stance for our religious liberty and be willing to pay the price. Even when others tell us it is a losing battle, or we might be tempted to raise the white flag, we don't give up the fight. We have to be strong enough to persevere in our goal and not let impatience lead to impotence.

It is estimated that a billion people are living under systems that suppress religious freedom. One billion! How can these countries live in peace, security and stability? Rays of hope can be found in Myanmar and Egypt. Where countries navigate toward democracy they tend to also work for religious freedom. Religious freedom is an essential centerpiece of human dignity, as it creates a climate of trust and encourages people of different religious traditions to work together in order to resolve problems.

Archbishop Carlo Maria Vigano, Apostolic Nuncio to the United States, gave a talk on November 12, 2012, at Notre Dame University, Indiana, entitled, "Religious Freedom, Persecution of the Church, and Martyrdom." He began by stating that there are a variety of ways religious freedom is threatened. Some are obvious and others more subtle, but just as dangerous. He said China, India, Pakistan and the region of the Middle East are countries where heavy and harsh burdens are imposed on Christians. He maintained that martyrdom is not limited to torture and death but also includes cases in which believers are ridiculed by non-believers who try to remove them from public manifestations of their beliefs. As a result, the believer remains but the faith disappears.

The Egyptian Salafists are now bold enough to burn churches, urge anti-Coptic riots and call for the expulsion of all Christians. Over 100,000 Copts have fled Egypt, and those who remain are willing to be martyrs— not in a violent way, but by giving witness. That is a sledgehammer fact. Many want to give Christian witness by providing and urging a non-violent struggle. Copts have organized marches near their cathedral commemorating how many of them have been killed. They symbolize a response to the Salafists who want an Islamist government and subordination or even expulsion of the Copts.[12]

In *The Seven Big Myths About the Catholic Church* Christopher Kaczor writes that much hostility toward particular Catholics and the wider Catholic Church is based on prejudices and ignorance. He believes it is a myth that religion and science are in conflict with each other; that the Church opposes freedom and happiness; that the Church hates women, homosexuals, the use of condoms to prevent HIV/AIDS; that celibacy causes the crisis of sexual abuse. His book deals with each of these myths, revealing the ways in which they are not true, that the Church is made of saints and sinners and those who govern it have made mistakes.

Many object that Catholics submit themselves to a patriarchal, archaic, and harmfully misogynistic institution that perpetuates scandals, conspiracies, and controversies. But Catholicism holds many precious and valuable things.

---

[12] Pinault, David. "Ready to be Martyrs," *America*. Vol. 207, No18, Dec. 2012, pp. 11-14.

One thinks of the tradition of the sacraments, the mystical writings and traditions—especially those that have been initiated or embodied by women—and social teaching that insists upon justice for all. G.K. Chesterton expressed it well when he stated that we possess a fanatical pessimism combined with a fanatical optimism.

In *Christianophobia: A Faith Under Attack* Rupert Shortt documents the fact that, since September 11, attacks on Christians have dramatically increased, especially in Muslim majority countries. A Muslim living in such countries will face harsh penalties and even death should their leaders discover that they have converted to Christianity. Iraq used to have over a million Christians, and now is the home of a mere 200,000.

If we want results we will need to pay the price, because better results require a higher price. Jesus said, "Much will be required of the person entrusted with much, and still more will be demanded of the person entrusted with more" (Lk 12:48). For the Christian, each acquired right implies a responsibility. Our tendency is to assert our rights without assuming our responsibilities. People who combine the two or who see and enact the relationship between the two are becoming more rare.

ORGANIZED CHRISTIANITY

Why are people leaving organized Christianity? Because we have not endorsed the costly, radical message of Jesus. He embodies a transforming, revolutionary love for all people. He reached out to the marginalized, renounced violence, loved not only close friends such as Martha, Mary and Lazarus, but also, and most strikingly, his enemies. He condemned hypocrisy, healed broken lives and invited all to embrace the kingdom of God. We often find excuses when confronted with his challenging, compelling, radical words. We might ask others to believe in him, but do we believe in him completely? Do we wish to appeal only to those aspects of Christianity that "feel good" and cost little to nothing? If so, can we rightly call ourselves Christians? Our words have to match our actions. Or, as we say, "walk the talk." Paul Wellstone, a senator from Minnesota, insists that we should never separate the lives we live from the words we speak.

Have we decided, as St. Paul encouraged us, to root our lives in love so we can be filled with the fullness of God (Eph 3:16-19)? This is a lifelong task ridden with courageous risks which many are not willing to "pay." Christ's love can overwhelm us, break open our hearts, animate our restricted vision. God's love exceeds and surpasses our knowledge and understanding. Once we grasp that love, our whole body can reverberate—like the turned up sound systems I often hear outside my window. We have a tendency to turn down the volume and muffle the words.

Organized Christianity can be very divisive due to various heated disagreements that have, to date, resulted in over forty-four thousand different denominations. But these divisions do not merely haunt Christianity at large. They exist within the Catholic church itself. John Allen Jr. believes that the United States is not polarized but tribalized. The different tribes are: pro-life Catholics, peace and justice Catholics, liturgical traditionalist Catholics, church reform Catholics, just to mention a few. The diversity can be a treasure but also create dysfunction, especially when the tribes become each others' enemies. We need to build zones of friendship with each other, where they can rub shoulders and debate issues in a respectful, civilized manner. The fights over same sex marriage, contraception, homosexuality, wages on. We need to move out of our comfort zones and embrace one another in love. By embracing prejudices instead of truth we demean God's love. As Catholics our attention should break through partisan and conventional lines so that we can be concerned about injustices like abortion, euthanasia, the death penalty, or why eighty percent of wealth in the last thirty years has gone to one percent of the population. If we focus only on abortion we can easily condone greed at the expense of the common good. If we focus *solely* on the conventional concerns of social justice we may become blind to the intrinsic dignity of life and the importance of a sound interior life.

Paul prayed that we might be strengthened in our inner being. Contrarily, our culture has wired us to our addictions. In fact, the pressures are so powerful that if we are to avoid the manifold addictions we need to put forth much discipline and hard work, not unlike that undertaken by our Olympic athletes who train long and hard for their event. We cannot just duck into a spiritual phone booth like Clark Kent and become a superman or a super woman.

Our age, according to Cardinal Thomas Collins, Archbishop of Toronto, is shaped by a "false wisdom" which is essentially opposed to the Catholic faith. Our costly mission is to make Christ known in our age *even though* our Catholic principles seem unattractive. He calls the superficial, attractive wisdom that may be peddled as "spiritual junk food," which can be delicious but not sustaining. We all swim in the popular and secularized culture that shapes our society. Relativism and individualism corrode the bonds of love, truth and peace. In the midst of this overwhelming pool, we need to build on the bedrock of prayer and our own conversion.

Cardinal Timothy Dolan asks John Allen Jr., and us, "Are we going to go back to the catacombs, or are we going to be in the market place?" My answer would be both, but we cannot give up on the *ad extra* evangelization of the culture, constantly coaxing, inviting, wooing, even flirting. We can't do that, of course, if we don't also tend to those within the fold. The people who are going to do all that have to be nurtured too."[13] We are not afraid to

13 Allen Jr., John. *A Pope of Hope*. New York, NY; Image Books, 2012, p.167.

wear a Packer or Brewer uniform or fashionable outfits with innumerable logos, but are we afraid to wear our Catholic faith?

A vast difference exists between being an "interested" Christian and a committed one. We are *interested* in knowing the price of commodities; are we committed to pay the price? The word "competent" comes from the root word "complete," and competent people are committed to excellence—they don't settle for average, but pay attention to details—they act or perform with consistency. People willing to pay the price do not gripe about how many sacrifices they need to endure. Discipline means doing things we don't like doing for the sake of something greater. If we are willing to do the small things, the larger ones will take care of themselves.

We might be able to discipline our thoughts and emotions, but to discipline our actions is even more challenging. Actions separate losers from winners. It is daunting to move ahead in spite of the odds against us. But we have plenty of inspiration from those who have faced and overcome those same odds. Paul grew inwardly as he paid the price outwardly. In his second letter to the Corinthians he wrote, "Therefore, we are not discouraged; rather, although our outer self is wasting away, our inner self is being renewed day by day" (2Cor. 4:16). Things might look like they are falling apart, but God is still present, giving us the strength and courage to face the future. So much of what we see here today is gone tomorrow, but what we don't see lasts forever.

We are weighed down by a materialistic, media-overdosed and celebrity-obsessed society. We need to ask, "what are the most real and valuable things in our lives?" In times of duress resulting from hurricanes, floods, fires and other natural disasters, people often discover what really counts, our loved ones. Destroyed homes can be rebuilt, material possessions can be replaced, or if not replaced at least let go of. But not loved ones. That is the reason why people rummaging through their ruined homes are not interested in electronic gadgets, silverware, precious jewelry, but family photographs, which are irreplaceable—reminders of past events, people who played important roles in our relationships. The snapshots create a collage of memories. We often forget that God plays a decisive role in the human relationships we value. God is the author of all human life and continues to help us to pay the price of loving others more and reaching out to those who have suffered from tragic hardships.

As Christians we need a spirit of joy, we need the Spirit to increase our joy, in part to counteract our difficulties, trials, and hardships. Our joy can increase as we prune the tentacles that secularism has wrapped around us, as we cut those things which promised joy, failed to deliver, but made their dwelling in us nevertheless. According to a recent study of 40,000 people, those who watch less television are happier. Why? Often simply because with fewer commitments to *my show,* they can spend more time with family and friends, more time actively reading or engaging in a hobby, all of which results in our being more satisfied with what we have. Shows are often filled with fluff—are literally "filler" to take up air time and gain ratings. Our families and friends cannot become the filler of our lives.

NEED TO SUCCEED

Advertising, and general cultural pressure, even from other Christians, can influence us to try and succeed at any cost. We can easily put ourselves ahead of everyone else. We witness this on a ground scale in wars and violence. Arnold Toynbee stated that "Nothing fails like success." What does this mean? We might be using an old approach to a challenge we are facing, and that old method is not working. When we have a challenge that is equal to the response, that is called success. Once we have a new challenge, the old, once successful response no longer works. Hence it is called a failure. He maintains that this statement usually summarizes all of history, because when challenges in life are met with equal responses we have success. But when challenges move to a higher level, or where it costs more, the once successful or old responses don't work. They fail.

The authors of *Crucial Conversations* studied over 2,200 projects, programs and their findings were stunning. They could accurately predict within ninety percent which projects and programs would fail months or a year in advance. The primary reason for failure was that people could not carry on crucial conversations. Put simply, they could not voice their disapproval or did not know what to do if there was a lack of leadership in their organization.[14] They had to learn to speak up at critical moments and hold fast to the idea that everyone was held accountable.

When asked about the length of the Afghanistan war, Captain Matthew Peterson replied, "So what? If it takes another 10, if that's the cost of success, then who cares how long it takes?"[15] Again, do we have this same attitude toward our spiritual maturation, or do we give up if we don't meet our goals within a short period of time? Many of us read articles and books filled with "how to succeed" skills. Perry Marshall, a successful salesperson, maintains there is a three step program to success: 1) find out the price 2) pay the price 3) get up and fall down. Notice that this method to success lacks any moral or spiritual framework. Our complete absorption in success often triumphs our personal relationships. We will succeed! Mission Accomplished! Satisfaction guaranteed! We become irritated when our destination or schedule is interrupted. We wait impatiently for the payoff and are afraid we will run out steam or passion. When we fail to succeed, how often we beat ourselves up, blame others or curse our circumstances. If we do succeed we pat ourselves on the back, revel in our satisfaction, and maybe set a loftier goal.

We need to be passionate and willing to pay the price to *do* the right thing rather than *gain* the right

[14] Kerry, Peterson, Joseph Grenny, Ron McMillan, Al Switzler. *Crucial Conversations*. New York, NY; McGraw Hill, p.12.

[15] *America*. Vol. 208, No. 2, Jan 21, 2013, from Raymond Scroth S.J. Book review *Into the Fire*, p.32.

things. Focusing on the present moment is often the best way to attend to the decisions we are making along our journey. Our attention should be on the quality of our decisions because they often will determine who we are becoming. Look upon interruptions as opportunities, not obstacles. Avoid becoming obsessed with achievement and focus more on the means by which we can avoid compromising our values, or neglecting our relationships. When we are less concerned about the payoffs and more about the journey we know we are on the right track.

WHAT IS THE PAYOFF?

Trapped in our enlightenment mentality, we link spiritual and emotional terms to our payoff. If we are willing to pay the price we will gain this or that reward. Is it possible to choose without a payoff? When we return from a vacation people often ask, "Did you have fun?" Why can't we just go on a vacation without producing fun? Tethered to the present moment means we are not thinking about a future payoff. We will face a higher cost if we choose collaboration and peace over competition and conflict. We need to replace the love of power with the power of love, a saying attributed to William Gladstone, a British Statesman.

Terry Hershey, who gives workshops on living balanced lives and healthy relationships, teaches that, "We are moved from wonderment to consumption. It becomes the very antithesis of beauty. There is an attempt to

Christianize it, by adding Jesus or God to the price tag."[16]
We are typically tempted by some sort of potential payoff,
"What's in it for me?" Amid the noise, it is critical that we
listen deeply and delve into the "ground of silence," as
Meister Eckhart wrote. Of course, this is challenging, but it
is not impossible. Many witnesses remind us that it can be
done. St. John of the Cross described it as "hearing silent
music." As the psalmist says, "Be still and confess that I
am God" (46:11).

When there is an empty space of time in our
calendars or planners we pay the price of filling it. Saying
"no" is difficult and challenging for many. We are willing
to pay a price for an orderly and controlled tomorrow or
even *today* but this seldom results in the orderly, put-
together life that we imagine. Do we give in to the urgency
of the moment at the expense of what is more important in
life? We are not always sure what we want in life, but we
are certain that we don't have it. We are so far from the
lady who was asked, "What is the best thing about being
104?" She replied, "No peer pressure."[17] Morris West
maintained that "It costs so much to be a full human being
that there are few who have the enlightenment or the
courage to pay the price."[18] "Every creature is a glistening,
glistening mirror of divinity," wrote Hildegard of Bingen.[19]

---

[16] Hershey, Terry. *The Power of Pause.* Chicago, IL; Loyola Press, 2009, p. 25.

[17] Ibid. p. 185.

[18] Ibid. p 206

[19] Ibid. p. 206.

Once we relate to others in this way we will be more willing to forgive.

Religious liberty is under constant attack. Intense opinions concerning organized Christianity can be divisive, and the pervasiveness of party politics leads to many heated discussions concerning abortion, euthanasia, death penalty, and many more controversial subjects. Debates that lead nowhere. Are we willing to pay the price of prudence, gauging our interactions based not on the possible payoff, but on the characteristics of charity?

This is complicated by the fact that many books on how to succeed in our society flood our bookstores, but often they lack a moral and spiritual framework. We are more interested in the payoff, "What's in for me?" rather than how we can put greater trust in God and helping others who are in much greater need.

FORGIVENESS

Books on the power of forgiveness are gaining popularity, almost an anomaly in the publishing industry. Some years ago I read an article entitled "Three Words that Heal." Those three words are: I forgive you. All of us experience hurts in our lives, not being appreciated, being made fun of, a cutting or sharp remark, or being betrayed. It is challenging to forgive someone, but if we do, we are no longer handcuffed to the person who hurt us.

Robin Casarjian was able to forgive the person who raped her. For some it is much easier to lug the resentment and revenge that can easily take control of our lives. Gabby Gifford is not resentful over all she has been through. "Why not," she was asked. She responded, "I want to move ahead!" Heather Abbott lost her left foot during the Boston Marathon bombing, but feels no malice toward the men accused of the crime. We might feel more in charge when we are angry and not merely "powerless." In actuality, forgiveness instills power in us whether the person "deserves it" or not. Some might feel weak if they forgive and demand that the other person say they are sorry, but this sort of contingency only complicates potential resentments and useless wrath. We need to pull the knife out of our gut if we have been passed over a promotion, if someone has been unfaithful to us, or if someone failed to invite us to a wedding. Scientific research has revealed that unforgiveness even takes a physical toll on us. It can result in high blood pressure, ulcers, heart failure or many other diseases. It might take some time to forgive, when we finally achieve a more merciful disposition we are at last able to see the other person with new lenses. We need to look to Jesus. He forgave Judas who betrayed him and called him friend, He forgave Peter, who denied three times that he even knew him. He forgave the good thief on the cross. Finally, and most poignantly, when he cried out, "Father, forgive them, they know what they are do," he forgave all of us (Lk 23:34).

In *Les Miserables* Bishop Bienvenu forgives Valjean who had spent nineteen years in prison for stealing a loaf of bread and has finally been released. The bishop offers him a place to stay, but Valjean takes silver objects from his home. Once he is caught by the police and brought before the Bishop, the latter tells the gendarmerie that he gave the criminal the silver, and proceeds to also offer him candlesticks! Valjean then strives to become what the bishop saw in him by dedicating himself to acts of kindness to the poor. His love now begins to spread out in concentric circles as he saves Fantine, a factory worker, from a prison sentence, adopts and raises an illegitimate daughter, Cossette, saves the life of Cossette's lover Marius, and forgives his nemesis Javert, the police official. The incredible thing about Valjean is that he refuses to stoop to his adversary's level and his heroism remains unknown to the bishop.

How many of us are fighting our battles with our enemies' weapons? It is challenging to respond with love where hate is the predominant force. Love in action is the best way to love our enemies, and especially the most powerful way to forgive them. The poison of rancor and hatred can seep into our spiritual groundwater. We are more concerned about shaping the world than in refining our own attitudes—especially toward racism and forgiveness. Dorothy Day maintained that we love God as much as the person we like or love least. When we think of the person who irks us the most, how forgiving are we? Can we authentically assume the attitude of Jesus on the cross? We also need forgiveness because people who love us will sometimes hurt us.

Pope Emeritus Benedict XVI visited his former butler, Paolo Gabriele, in the Vatican police barracks after he had been convicted. He told Paolo that he was forgiven for allowing Vatican documents to be leaked out.

In *A Knock at the Door* Wayne Bisek recounts troubled incidents from his childhood. His mother told her husband that Wayne was not his child. His tyrant father disowned him as his own son. He lived in a dysfunctional family where anger and pain were constantly present, a home of incestuous rape where his father often beat him with a leather strap. Everything that Wayne aspired for was taken away from him because he lived in constant fear, frustration and violence. Many of his feelings were grounded in revenge and hatred. After much struggle, however, Wayne was willing to extend the olive branch and was able to pay the price of forgiving his father. He invited him back into his life at the birth of A.J. his first son. Now he sees life as filled with love, happiness and peace. Loving others in spite of their faults, shortcomings, imperfections, but because of them, demands the highest kind of love which some find too costly a price to pay.

Yes, it is dangerous and costly to live our Christian principles and values today, to endorse the costly, radical message of Jesus to "love your enemies, do good to those who hate you, bless those who curse you, pray for those who mistreat you" (Lk 6:27-28). Are we willing to pay the price as so many martyrs and saints did? Above all, to be able to forgive others and ourselves, we need a good dosage of trust in a loving and compassionate God.

SCRIPTURE PASSAGES FOR REFLECTION

"Do you not know that we who were baptized into Christ
Jesus were baptized into his death?"

(Rom 6:3)

"Much will be required of the person entrusted with much,
and still more will be demanded of the person entrusted
with more."

(Lk 12:48)

"That Christ may dwell in your hearts through faith, and
that you be rooted and grounded in God."

(Eph 3:17)

"Therefore we are not discouraged; rather, although our
outer self is wasting away, our inner self is being renewed
day by day."

(2 Cor 4:16)

"Father, forgive them, they know not what they do."

(Lk 23"34)

QUESTIONS TO CONSIDER

1. What would you be willing to die for?
2. How can you take a strong stand for religious freedom?
3. How can you make Christ better known despite the
   relativism and individualism in our society?
4. What are the most valuable things in your life?
5. Do you get trapped in the payoff, or "What's in for
   me?" How do you counteract this?

CHAPTER FOUR
WHOM CAN WE TRUST?

A parent can easily identify with the image from Isaiah, in which a mother never forgets but selflessly nurses her child, "Can a mother forget her own infant, be without tenderness for the child of her womb" (49:15)? What an intimate and close bond is forged between mother and child. This female image of God can shock some of us. But can you imagine a better metaphor of God's total commitment to us than a mother suckling a new born child? Once a mother tried to explain nursing to her infant child. The daughter responded, "But she's drinking milk in the living room!" It might be difficult to find a more touching comparison because it perfectly embodies the complete gift of oneself. The bond spells out, in bold relief, **T-R-U-S-T**.

Trust in God is never in vain, but if we are going to live the Christian life to the fullest we will pay a high degree of trust. In the Book of Isaiah we find a startling contrast of lament and comfort when Israel cries out that she is forsaken and desolate. We see this all around us in those people today who, feeling the same way, raise their complaints to God, people who are unable to find jobs, others who are finding it hard to make ends meet in our teetering economy, and still others whose lives have been destroyed by floods, earthquakes, hurricanes, and other natural disasters. It is challenging to trust God under those trying circumstances. How can we trust God in the midst of pain and trial? Whom can we trust these days? Lack of faith, lack of trust, has become real problems in our society. Pope Emeritus Benedict XVI, while not aloof to the state of the world, insisted that worldly fears can be overcome by trusting in God. In his letter *Door of Faith* he stated that "Faith grows when it is lived as an experience of love received and when it is communicated as an experience of grace and joy."[20]

Trust and faith are in a sense uncanny, extraordinary signs of contradiction in a skeptical age. Let us return to the metaphor of mother and child, that scriptural image which is also extraordinary because people were living in a patriarchal society where the father was the head. A mother nursing a child is indeed startling because of its feminine nature. We can consider the case of the teacher who asked some small children who God is. A boy piped up and said, "God is whatever you think he is, but he is not a girl!" Even the child was scandalized by the possibility of God's feminine dimensions. And yet the mother and child metaphor brings out the intimacy God wants with us as well as the powerful ways in which God sustains us. God certainly sustained the Israelites out in the desert by giving them the manna each day.

20

Benedict XVI, Pope. "Porta Fidei." http://www.vatican.va/holy_father/benedict_xvi/motu_proprio /documents/hf_ben-xvi_motu-proprio_20111011_porta-fidei_en.html. 5/13/2013.

Nevertheless, not unlike children, and not unlike us, they started to complain. The amazing challenge of trust that God set before them came in the fact that they were to take enough food just for the day. We can imagine them asking like we might, "What if God forgets tomorrow?" But God doesn't— and not only does God *not* forget them but God gives them quail. We hear or read about stories where mothers abandon their children, or, tragically kill them. The image of the unconditional mother can be imperfect, but God will never abandon any of us:"Because you are precious in my sight, and honored, and I love you" (Is. 43:4). We see this in the book of Daniel. Shadrach, Meschach, Abednego, three Israelite men, were thrown in the fiery furnace because they refused to worship a false god. In spite of the fiery flames, which could easily have filled them with fear, they experienced the calm that comes only through radical trust. They remained faithful to God regardless of the cost (Dan 3). In the midst of our present crisis we certainly need that level of trust. In the Hebrew Scriptures God is often described as a rock, a stronghold of stability which is needed in time of uncertainty. And yet Prudential Life Insurance, which is subject to the vagaries of the market, may one day find its rock worn down, even though it has stood as the Rock of Gibraltar, one of the most recognized symbols in the world. God is our rock. When we are on the rock of God we are steady even when sprayed by the sea-foam of trials.

Jesus challenges us to absolute loyalty which requires trust. We cannot serve two masters. Wealth can be an engaging rival to our commitment and trust in Jesus. Do we truly believe that earthly goods will never surpass heavenly realities? We hear this often, but do we really trust God more than our insurance company? The trap and temptation set for us does not consist in having money, but in an inordinate attachment to wealth and possessions which many fall into. Materialism exercises a certain tyranny when people pursue nothing more than material goods and money. Ronald Rolheiser contends that we have to give our money away if we are going to be healthy. Jesus also encourages us to trust in God's goodness and providence. Using natural examples he contrasts our need for food to the birds of the air. They neither sow or reap or gather into barns like we do. Yet God takes care of them. Our challenge is to trust that God will take care of us. Jesus also compares our need for clothing to the lilies of the field. They certainly do not work for their "clothing," and yet look at them: they are more beautiful than Solomon's kingdom. When Queen Sheba saw his great palace, "she was breathless" (I Kgs 10:5). Yet, Jesus said, "I tell you that not even Solomon in all his splendor was clothed like one of these" (Mt 6:29). If God takes care of the birds and lilies how much more ourselves? We have to stop living in a vacuum and make these sayings of Jesus a vessel for our beliefs, paying the price.

All of this said, our response might be, "Easier said than done." Isn't it fascinating that we trust in a compass, in scientists discovering cures for various diseases, labels on cans, people driving on the right side of the road? In these and so many other ways we trust others, even if it is with caution. Do we treat God with the same caution?. We carry the worm of mistrust.

Intellectually, we admit that God knows what is best for us. But to practice unconditional trust demands much humility, which means that the one being trusted knows better than we do. Trust implies we often don't understand what is happening. We become like Mary who, witnessing seemingly providential and simultaneously confusing events, "kept all these things, reflecting on them in her heart" (Lk 2:19).

Psychologists speak of "liminal experiences" where we become more aware of God's presence in the extraordinary transitional moments that interrupt the mundane situations in our lives. Examples might be: the birth of a child, falling in love, watching a sunset, forgiving someone who has hurt us, reaching out to a homeless person. This is how we can encounter God in our ordinary faith experiences. They can happen suddenly: Abram, who was called by God to leave his homeland; Moses, who was tending sheep, experiences God in the burning bush; Mary, who was invited by Gabriel to be the mother of God; Peter and the other Apostles, who were going about the daily business of fishing responding to, "Follow me." St. Paul assures us that, "Faith comes from what is heard" (Rom 10:17). Faith is a loving response to what God wants of us, but we have to be willing to pay the price. Can we discern a difference between faith and trust? One possible explanation is that faith is a noun, something we possess, whereas trust is a verb, something we do. For many it is easier to have faith in God but harder to exercise trust in God, because we have set our anxieties and worries into a battle with our trust. Winning this battle can be costly.

ANXIETY AND WORRY

The opposite of faith is not doubt or atheism, but anxiety. Some of us have a cascade of problems which make inroads into our lives, causing anxiety and worry. St. Peter encourages us, "Cast all your worries upon him because he cares for you" (1 Pt. 5:7). We too easily become anxious and worry what is going to happen to us, our family, our future. We relieve our anxiety through pursuit of fame, success, financial security, power and sex. If we have financial security, we soon become concerned about protecting it, and if we have power we look over our shoulders because we fear that we will lose it. Worry is one of the most useless emotions. Worry has been described as interest paid on trouble before it is due. What do we gain by it except high blood pressure, ulcers, and heart conditions? Worry comes from an old English word which means "to choke." It will choke us spiritually and sometimes physically. Worry also causes frustration and sleepless nights, like the man who had to take a flight to England during the Icelandic volcano eruption. He worried his flight would get held up for days and that, even if he got to England, the volcano would erupt again stranding him for days or longer. Or what if he got caught in an ash plume and his plane crashed? Needless to say, he survived the round trip. The anticipation is usually worse than the realization.

Worry is a way by which we try to live the future today. But we *invent* the future before it actually happens, and, if we are anxious, we tend to shade it with grim colors. Worry does not take away tomorrow's troubles; it takes away today's peace. Jesus exhorted us, "Do not worry about tomorrow; tomorrow will take care of itself. Sufficient for a day is its own evil" (Mt 6:34). We will not die from an unanswered question. Often we would rather worry than pray because we are more familiar with worry. Worry can be an internal fire that blazes, but offers very little warmth. Are we like Jack-in-the-boxes? Turn the crank and we hear music and suddenly Jack jumps out. Indeed worry can turn the crank and cause many knee-jerk reactions. Many of our thoughts are driven or even consumed by our worries. Robert Wicks, a therapist and famous author, insists that if you told him what you are thinking about most he could tell you who your god/God is—and it is not always Christ, at least not first and foremost. Jesus said, "For where your treasure is, there also will your heart be" (Mt. 6:21). What do we think about most?

We often try to tie God's hands and become anxious about the "fact," which in truth is an illusion, that God's hands are tied. We do this rather than put our lives into God's hands. Why is it, because the latter is costly and daring. We cherry pick our trust in God. If God did everything for us immediately, how would we learn trust and patience? Trust can only exist if we accept the fact that some questions will remain unanswered, and that we must live with uncertainty and ambiguity. Isn't "In God We Trust" the official motto of the United States? It was first put on a two cent coin in 1864, a proclamation followed on other coins. It became an Act of Congress in 1956. Do we believe and live that motto in our lives? Jesus extends that invitation to us.

Of course, we worry, nor should we grow discouraged when we do, because even some of the great saints worried. St. Therese of Lisieux worried a lot, but finally realized she had to put all her trust in a loving God. Francis de Sales worried that he was damned and suffered a nervous breakdown, but had to learn to trust God more. And he did. Alphonse Liquori was afflicted with scruples and was exiled from his own community. Hildegard of Bingen use to worry about her sins and then finally realized that she did not have enough time to be concerned about them.

Oliver Wendell Holmes maintained that our greatest act of faith consists in finally finding out we are not God. Remember how the serpent tricked Eve and Adam: "You certainly will not die." The basic sin is "you will be like gods" (Gen 3:4-5). St. Paul assures us that "The one who is righteous by faith will live" (Rom 1:17). We are made right in God's sight through faith. Our holiness will grow and wax stronger by the exercise of our faith. When we are righteous, faith becomes the rock-foundation of our lives. This way of living is certainly embodied in many elderly people. The intense love that the saints had for God was based on their faith, which put them in constant contact with the Divine and can do the same for us. Elaborating upon the words of Jesus, Thomas Aquinas, believed that a house would not exist without a solid foundation. That foundation must be faith. Other virtues like love and hope might be more admirable, but they would not exist without faith, which always has a price tag attached to it.

NEED FOR FAITH

John Allen Jr. argues that if there were someone to dream up a program which could potentially draw sixty-eight million U.S. Catholics into a deeper practice of their faith it would be hailed as a missionary bonanza, and yet Churches spend much of their energies planning ways to address much more superficial and even petty concerns. The book of Hebrews tells us that without faith it is impossible to please God (11:6). St. John Chrysostom and St. Augustine repeat the same idea. St. Augustine believed that faith is the *beginning* of our salvation. St. Francis Xavier, the outstanding missionary, taught that it is not the physical exertion or the nature of the task that helps us to progress, but our spirit of faith. A living and active faith is concerned about all creation because if we truly believe in God, by implication we believe that we are custodians of it and each other. In faith, then we need to be concerned about our crumbling infrastructure, inadequate schools, lack of jobs, violence and greed. Many spiritual writers use the image of God playing a hide and seek game with us. God can be hidden behind even tragic events, which often bewilder and confuse us. We need to throw the searchlight of our faith on these events despite the veil concealing their meaning. That is the cost of living our faith. Faith enables us to view the whole universe, its myriad galaxies, and all its events as a huge monstrance revealing a Triune God.

When looking at our earth, we need to remember it took 14 billion years to form it. When looking at the skies or the universe, we can say with the psalmist, "When I see your heavens, the work of your fingers, the moon and the stars that you set in place? What are humans that you are mindful of them, mere mortals that you care for them?" (8:4-5). Truly all of this is a deep mystery. As Ilio Delia states, "All of us want to own a piece of the mystery, claim it as our own, defend it like property, and fight for it at all costs."[21] Too often we look at the universe and all of life with cocked eyebrows, or we hone ourselves into a frail and fickle nature rather than realizing we are humans loved by God.

Faith is more concerned with courage than heroism, because it urges us to pray even when things look pointless or useless. When no answers are available or forthcoming amidst our confusions and frustrations, we need to rely on our faith in God. Defeat and death will be

21 Delio. *The Emerging Christ*, p.138.

conquered by our strong faith. Faith holds tenaciously to God's promises and helps us to climb any mountain from which, if we follow through, we are rewarded with a panoramic view that can be breath taking.

We might question what God had in mind when designing our aging process. Isn't it ironic that when we reach the age of maturity, our bodies start falling apart? We are in a pitched battle with aging through the unexpected turns as we navigate through its many jungles. Faith plays an extremely important role as we age, but doesn't always provide us with ready-made answers. Ronald Rolheiser believes we are paying a high price by working so hard to create a world that tries to deny, delay and disguise aging. Elders are put into separate homes, tucked away from the mainstream of life. Some are given lackluster support. Euthanasia, which defines life purely by utility, is making inroads. As we age we might not be very productive, but we are more reflective. Older people are our wisdom figures; they are examples of character honed by many years of sorrow and joy. They, as well as we, need to face the reality of death, which is always challenging and demands the price of our faith. By faith we know that death is the outward sign of what is going on inside of us. Karl Rahner believed that the high point of our lives is death. At the end of his life, Jesus cried out, "Into your hands I commend my spirit" (Lk 23:46). When dying, St. Francis of Assisi said, "Welcome sister death." In *Studying the Life of Saint Francis of Assisi* Bill Hugo, a fellow

Capuchin, states that part of studying Francis' life is to deepen our own faith life.[22]

An airplane's compass defies all our senses: we cannot see, hear, touch, taste or smell it. But a pilot knows it's there because he sees the results. He can look at an instrument in the cockpit and see that his compass is pointing in a certain direction. The pilot has faith that it is correct and stakes his life and the lives of his passengers on its accuracy. Our faith is our spiritual compass. It also defies our senses, but it will guide us to our destination.

Liminal space might be an apt metaphor here. *Liminal* refers to an in-between space, a neither-here-nor-there. Think of the time when one lets go and one is caught. This is the liminal moment of faith. It is the time to let go of what we are hanging on to have faith that one will be caught. Often I encourage others by saying, "Hang in there!" Mary's "Yes," to what God asked of her implies an unspoken process of letting go. She had to pay the price of becoming pregnant even as Joseph did not know how this was accomplished. But, in response to Mary's yes and Joseph's humility, God reveals to Jesus' foster father that this was done through the power of the Holy Spirit. When we live in this liminal space we often are confused, even upset, but we need to trust God as Mary did. The howling dirge of disaster usually precedes the shouted alleluias.

Mary always did God's will. Spiritual writer Anthony Bloom states that "We must also remember that when we fulfill God's will...we must not do it tentatively,

---

[22] Hugo, William. OFM Cap. *Studying the Life of St. Francis of Assisi*, 2nd Ed. Hyde Park, New York; New City Press, 2011, p.109.

thinking of putting it to the test, to see what comes of it, because then it does not work. We must outgrow this attitude, be prepared to do God's will and pay the cost. Unless we are prepared to pay the cost, we are wasting our time."[23]

Pope Emeritus Benedict XVI has alerted us to the ways in which atheism has made inroads in our world. There is a form of atheism which considers our religious beliefs as irrelevant and useless to our daily existence. As a result, people's belief in God is superficial and they live as if God does not exist. He insists that to remedy this we need to carefully contemplate nature, where God is ever present. As St. Augustine assured us, the Lord is closer to us than we are to ourselves. And yet, close as God is, only faith can allow this closeness to come to life. Faith can transform our value judgments, our choices and our concrete actions provided we are willing to pay the price of living it to the fullest.

PEOPLE OF FAITH

Barbara Joose of Cedarburg, WI has written 43 highly acclaimed children's books over the last thirty years. She said that some times it might take five hundred revisions of a book and years to produce one, and six years to find a publisher. One of her most successful books is *Mama, Do You Love Me?* which celebrates a parent's unconditional love for a child despite all the challenges a parent faces. She insists that her faith has sustained her during all this. Joose maintains that she is Catholic to the

---

[23] Garvey, John. *Modern Spirituality.* Springfield, Illinois; Template, 1985, pp. 34-35.

bone, and finds the Mass is a way to deepen her faith and spirituality. She also says that there are things in Catholicism that you cannot see, but which you know are present anyway: that's faith.

If we believe that God created the earth, this faith can urge us to be better custodians. One day while Sharen Trembath of Angola, New York, walked along Lake Erie she spotted a dialysis bag on the shoreline. She became very upset because this was the twentieth one she had seen there. Sharen is an avid environmentalist and finds it difficult to understand how people can treat all that God has created in this way. Her deep faith inspired her to begin "Great Lakes Beach Sweep" bolstered by her family and friends. Over twenty-six years she has attracted some twenty-six hundred volunteers to donate two hours once a year to restore ninety-five miles of shoreline.

What people collected should amaze and disturb us: Styrofoam products, detergent bottles, some 136 tires at one time. Sharen has done this without any grant money, funding or salary. She insists that if God, who said, after creating the world said, "It is good," then we need to help keep a clean world. Her faith motivates her to a deep sense of gratitude for all God has created, and she is willing to pay the price of her time to this project.

Sister Nancy Kehoe, a Sacred Heart sister and clinical psychologist, works to reveal the ways in which faith issues were ignored thirty years ago when the medical profession deals with mental illness, and work to redress this wrong. Thirty years ago talking about faith issues was considered distracting and scientifically problematic, because, according to common wisdom, patients used it as a defense mechanism. If they spoke of faith, the theory went, they were hiding something deeper. What she has learned in ministering to them is that their faith has become their inner strength. Sister Nancy has organized a group who want to talk about their mental illness and religion. People who struggle with mental illness feel isolated and often keep others at a distance, or have difficulty holding a job. We need to create safe environs where people can talk about their illness and allow their faith to heal them. In *Porta Fidei* Pope Emeritus Benedict XVI states that "Faith without charity bears no fruit...faith and charity each require the other."[24]

Emile Griffin, author of *Green Leaves for Later Years*, would have written a very different story had not her faith been in tact. Griffin, who suffers from crippling rheumatoid arthritis, had to recalibrate her understanding of aging.[25] She notes how important Christian faith is in the aging process, insists that it is only through faith that our leaves can stay green even in our advanced years. She uses Jeremiah's saying about trusting in the Lord, "is like a tree planted beside the waters that stretches out its roots to the stream: it fears not the heat when it comes, its leaves stay green" (17: 8).

[24] Benedict XVI, Pope. "Porta Fidei." http://www.vatican.va/holy_father/benedict_xvi/motu_proprio/documents/hf_ben-xvi_motu-proprio_20111011_porta-fidei_en.html. 5/13/2013.

[25] Griffin, Emile. *Green Leaves for Later Years*. Downers Grover, IL; InterVarsity Press, 2012.

FAITH THAT IS TESTED

My faith was tested recently after an ice storm here in Milwaukee, Wisconsin. I was scheduled for an 8:45 Mass on the east side of the city. Thinking that I could easily scrape the ice off my car in ten minutes, I went outside at eight o'clock. It took me close to a half hour. When I arrived at the parish at 8:40, because they have limited parking, there was no parking space. I drove around the block and found a place near an alley entrance, but I partially blocked it. Then I was afraid that I would receive a ticket. When I arrived in the sacristy, the deacon was very helpful in calming me down as I vested. I have a penchant for starting Mass on time, but failed in my efforts this time. After Mass, I was told that another Mass was scheduled for me at a neighboring parish, something I did not know about. To complicate matters, the directions that were given me how to get there were wrong. I ended up going in the opposite direction. I stopped and asked a man who was scraping off his car where the parish was and he told me how to drive down such and such a street, turn left for one block, and go one more block, and take a right. But then he decided to lead me with his car. Thank God for Good Samaritans! This Mass did start on time. God was testing my faith: it was as though God was saying, "Do you trust me?"

We need a faith that has sunk deep into the marrow of our bones. Those who wrote the scriptures are instructive in this manner. Their faith seems to effuse from the very core of their being. "Keep our eyes fixed on Jesus, the leader and perfecter of faith" (Hebrews 12:2). "Consider it all joy when you encounter various trials, for you know that the test of your faith produces perseverance" (James 1:2). Regretfully, many "Christians" are losing their faith in the sacred nature of scripture. Faced with a vast array of religions, Christian, Jewish, Muslim, Buddhist, Hindu and many others, some Americans are making the choice not to choose because so much is up for grabs. We are in the midst of swift social and technological changes that we have never seen before. We need ground under our feet to know our own identity so we can navigate these shifty changes that swirl around us. Jesus still remains the answer inviting us to deeper faith and trust in him and not counting the cost. St. Peter wrote "In this you rejoice, although now for a little while you may have to suffer through various trials, so that the genuineness of your faith, more precious than gold that is perishable even tested by fire, may prove to be for praise, glory and honor at the revelation of Jesus Christ" (I Pt. 1:6-7). This is the price we pay.

In *Christianophobia: A Father Under Attack*, Rupert Shortt illuminates the fact that faith has mobilized millions of people to work for democracy, support human rights and eliminate suffering. At the same time, the fall of Hosni Mubarak in Egypt did not result in any relief for the Christians there. Faith can bring about good things, can be instrumental in changing the social order for the better, but it is fundamentally other-worldly. Although this can give rise to many difficulties, the other-worldly aim of faith also guides us when the good things we wish for are withheld.

The film *Life of Pi* is about a sixteen year old Indian boy's passage on a freighter to a new life in America. His voyage ends in a shipwreck. The film vividly depicts how he responded to life despite all his intense suffering. His life is comparable to Job's because he loses his parents and brother in the shipwreck, endures many months lacking human companionship, sustains starvation, injury and thirst. But he does not lose his faith. Pi is even grateful to God for his gift of life, the universe around him and especially the animals like the Bengal tiger. The film helps us see things through Pi's creative and open mind. The breaking point comes when Pi has nothing to give, no strength left, no understanding why these horrible things happened to him. He finally gives himself over totally to God. The film tries to put some order in the chaos and despair that many of us experience.

Dietrich Bonhoeffer was certainly a faith-witness to Christ. Because of his baptismal commitment, he was not afraid to criticize the Nazi regime. He was imprisoned in a concentration camp and died a martyr's death at the age of 39. He contended that a Christian must not only *profess* his faith in Jesus but must *make this profession by living it daily*. That is the price one has to pay. When others were silent he spoke out, asking church leaders, "Where is Abel, your brother?" Bonhoeffer was shocked that they did not speak out against the Third Reich's crimes. He challenged them to embrace the costly grace of their baptism. He believed too many drank the deadly poison of false compromise, which killed their courage and prevented them from following Christ amidst an awful crisis.

When Hitler occupied Austria in 1938, all men were ordered to enlist in the army. Franz Jagerstatter, a farmer and father of four, consented to military training but refused to fight in Hitler's army. That insured his execution. His pastor, neighbors and even the Bishop tried to convince Franz to fight for the sake of his family. But he insisted that his faith and strong convictions compelled him to follow his conscience and not the Third Reich. He was imprisoned and executed on August 9, 1943, at the age of 36. The Vatican declared him a martyr and placed him on the path to sainthood. His deep faith and courage remains an inspiration for many to say no to war, especially unjust war, and to desire peace at any price. To arrive at this particular point in his life meant paying the price of deepening his faith every day, and to open himself to ongoing conversion, which is indeed challenging.

SCRIPTURE PASSAGES FOR REFLECTION

"Can a mother forget her own infant, be without tenderness for the child of her womb?"

(Is 49:15)

"Do not worry about tomorrow, tomorrow will take care of itself."

(Mt. 6:34)

"Cast all your worries upon him because he cares for you."

(1 Pt 5:7)

"For where your treasure is, there also will your heart be."

(Mt. 6:21)

"The one who is righteous by faith will live."

(Rom 1:17)

QUESTIONS TO CONSIDER

1. How do you increase your trust in God and make it unconditional?
2. How do you counteract anxiety and worry?
3. Do you believe that God can be hidden in tragic events? How?
4. How has faith transformed your values and choices?
5. Has your faith been tested and did you react?

CHAPTER FIVE
COSTLY CONVERSION

Too often conversion is considered as "getting rid of something" in order that something else can take its place. Costly conversion, however, means getting rid of everything within us that prevents us from being filled with the Holy Spirit. It is a change that comes deep within us, not a superficial, but a radical change through listening to Jesus and his invitation to repent and commit ourselves to the Gospel. Giving money to the poor or being kind cannot substitute for spiritual change. As praiseworthy as this is, it is not conversion, because we can afford to do it. Real conversion is putting away something that we *are:* our prejudices, biases, resentments, or habits that have become an intimate part of us. Conversion is one of the most intense forms of asceticism. The Vatican placed it at the heart of ecumenism and Pope John Paul II reiterated this enunciation. Raymond Brown calls it a *metanoia,* a complete change of attitudes, fixed ideas or ways of living. It is not a rearranging or dusting of furniture but a *complete* house cleaning. Conversion is the touchstone of our spirituality. Paul Tillich says that it consists in being grasped by the ultimate concern. It is an internal transformation wherein God becomes the center of our lives.

Conversion is usually preceded by restlessness or dissatisfaction. Perhaps this is because we will not change unless some discontentedness drives us to do so. St. Francis of Assisi spent a year in a Perugian prison as a prisoner of war, a privation which directly affected his later conversion. David O'Rourke suggests that we will not turn from the road we are on unless "we hit bottom." Of course, we can easily resist the inner ache that persists. Rosemary Haughton believes that one of our general pathological fears is resistance to change. Moses resisted the invitation from God in the burning bush, but this burning bush became a consuming fire that propelled him to go to Pharaoh and ask him to let God's people go. Jeremiah, Isaiah, and Jonah resisted God's invitation to be prophets. At Saul's conversion, Ananias resisted the Lord's request that he take care of Saul. Augustine prayed that he might become chaste but not right away. We can procrastinate, a phenomenon described by some writers as the devil's chloroform. Should our initials be TNT? Tomorrow, but not today! Or are we are just too lazy to scale to new heights because we are afraid of what God might ask of us?

Most of us have a strong desire to see the future before it happens. Even though we dislike surrendering the steering wheel of life, much of what happens is out of our control. Such surrender often demands the conversion that puts mind over matter: if you really don't mind, it doesn't matter. For some, however, everything matters. Very few things live up to our expectations. The cost of letting go of a loved one or some material things will draw massive amounts from our reserves, and this often changes us significantly. Out of death comes life. From the womb to the tomb all life is a letting go. We need to wait for that which will come with rebirth, to patiently await the point at which a caterpillar becomes a butterfly, for just like nature, we cannot hurry the process. Heraclitus, a pre-Socratic and one of the first philosophers, insisted that we cannot step into the same river twice. Changes are what keep us alive. Change is woven into the fabric of our lives and the canvas of universe. As the famous folk saying goes, "If you want God to smile, just tell God your plans." God's words to Isaiah drive this point home, "For my thoughts are not your thoughts, nor your ways my ways" (55:8).

John Cardinal Newman believed that if we are to live well we need to change often, as this will enable us to live life more fully. If we fail to do so, we might spend much of our lives as the "living dead." This is illustrated by a sign on a tombstone which read, Born 1890, Died 1970, Lived 40 years. Too often we resist change, or make all the wrong changes while we remain stubborn in the areas that most need conversion. It is hard to give up the toys of our childhood. Some walk lock step in their own tight-fisted rigidity and refuse to change. One of the paradoxes of our human condition is that we long for God's or someone else's love, but before we can allow the love to flow into our lives, we need to make some fundamental change. I once advised a religious sister friend to allow God to love her even more. This really helped her increase her own love for others. Too often we shrink from receptivity of God's love, considering ourselves unworthy. We have a strong tendency to be autonomous, wanting to control our lives, the lives of others, and even God. The Pharisee of the Gospel is an example of someone who refused to be loved by God, because his life was too taken up with himself: he thanked God that he was not like the rest of the people.

All of this being said, even if we do not cooperate with the graces of conversion, God continues to search after us. Each day we are given many opportunities for conversion, so we have to grease the skids of those graces. Some cases are harder than others, but *none* are without hope. In the *Lord of the Rings* the wizard Gandalf considers the problematic character of Gollum and states, "I have not much hope that Gollum can be cured before he dies, but there is a chance of it."[26] As Christians, we believe that "for God all things are possible" (Mt. 19:26).

PEOPLE WHO CONVERTED

In recent times many have converted to the Catholic faith. The list includes but is not limited to: Mortimer Adler, Nathaniel Hawthorne's daughter, Rose, who became a nun, Robert Hugh Benson, G. K. Chesterton, Joyce Kilmer, John Henry Newman, Kateri Tekawitha, Gary Cooper, Clare Booth Luce, Faye Dunaway, Evelyn Waugh, Bill Veeck, Dorothy Day, Thomas Merton, Scott Hahn, Robert Bork, and Tony Blair.

The average number of Americans who join the Catholic Church on Holy Saturday comes to around 150,000. The reasons are many: some are inspired by

---

[26] Winright, Tobias. "Gandalf, Gollum, and the Death Penalty," *Sojourners*. Vol. 42, No I, January, 2013, p. 26.

family members who are Catholic, others join after exploring different faith groups, and still others find the rich Catholic tradition and teachings attractive. In the midst of uncertain and turbulent times, some find the Catholic Church to be a true and solid anchor. The Rite of Christian Initiation of Adults is a process of conversion through which those interested in the Catholic faith study it. People who act as sponsors often speak of their own conversion, which can sometimes spur even greater *metanoia*.

In *Natural Cures Revealed* Kevin Trudeau writes about his trying experience as a convicted felon. He readily admits to two felonies which happened over twenty years ago. In his youth, he bounced two checks and put false information on several credit cards when applying for them. Kevin took responsibility for his mistakes, but made the restitution and spent two years in prison. He paid the price, but turned his life around, in part because he did not blame others but started by blaming himself.[27]

Jeanne Jugan, a French peasant woman, was converted by the plight of the poor. She started a religious order known as the Little Sisters of the Poor. A few years after she founded her order, a priest was appointed as chaplain to oversee the community. Once he saw her in action, he had her transferred to another convent, where she instructed novices. Jugan lived in an obscurity that bordered on anonymity. Eventually the chaplain died.

---

[27] Trudeau, Kevin. *Natural Cures Revealed.* Westmont, Il; Alliance Publishing Group, 2006, p. 31.

Jeanne also died, but at the time of her passing many of the sisters who lived with her did not know that she who emptied bedpans and swept floors was actually the foundress of their community. It wasn't until eleven years later that the truth was revealed. Jeanne never told anyone, complained, fought back, became upset, or demanded credit. She was willing to pay the price of obscurity with humility and obedience, and she offered no resistance. Jeanne paid the price, and her conversion was therefore more complete.

In a similar way, once we overcome any resistance, we are ready to surrender to the Lord. We are more open to God's will over our own. Sometimes this requires that we learn more fully who God is. Job initially withstood the trial of losing all his property and his ten children and was able to accept his suffering. But later he experienced months of misery and emptiness, many sleepless nights, wondering where God was in all that happened. He gradually came to affirm God's control over all things, and lowered himself in humble submission to the heavy blows he received. Job finally acknowledges God's supremacy, power and justice, where the God of hearsay becomes the God of experience. Francis of Assisi's conversion enabled him to surrender all his clothes to his father and to embrace the leper whom he had he shunned for some time. He later admitted that what before seemed bitter was changed into sweetness of body and soul. In the chapel of San Damiano he heard the crucifix above the altar say to him "Repair my house." In the chapel of the Angels, the

Portziuncula, on the feast of St. Mathias in 1208, he heard proclaimed the Gospel about Jesus sending out his Apostles to preach. Struck by these words, he declared that this is what he wished for, what he sought after, and what he wanted to do. According to his first biographer, Thomas of Celano, these events had a deep and profound effect on his conversion.

Surrender is accompanied by a new vision. As the book of Proverbs states, "Without vision the people perish" (29:18). For Moses it was the vision to lead the Israelites out of slavery. Jeanne Jugan had a vision of humility, which allowed her to accept her lowly state. Francis of Assisi struggled with his vision to, in the words that Christ spoke to him, *"Repair my house,"* and gradually through his conversion realized that the greater battle was inside himself, not on the official battlefield. That battle could be won without the use of arms.

In more recent times, Caroline Herring left for China, where she taught English classes right after she finished college. A fellow missionary grew to like her, and asked if she would be willing to leave her air conditioned room equipped with a toilet and join them. They lived in a a dirty and crowded bath-house that had nothing more than a few ceiling spigots. Caroline agreed to pay the price of leaving her comfortable quarters, because she felt this would help her better understand what it meant to be part of her fellow human beings. Her preconceived ideas of the Trinity disappeared, and she could feel the Holy Spirit moving among her companions, because they were so kind to each other. Herring admits that this experience changed her life. She was humbled and had a whole new idea of who God is, of the purpose of religion and of service. She even wrote a song about conversion entitled, "China." Herring has now become a famous social justice singer and songwriter.[28]

R.A. Dickey, now a pitcher for the Toronto Blue Jays, had to deal with both the experience of being sexually abused at the age of fourteen, *and* overcoming a near death encounter when he tried swimming across the Missouri River. The undertow almost killed him, but just before taking his last breath Dickey was able to propel himself upward. That experience changed his life. He started caring about his wife, children and his knuckle-ball pitching. In 2012, Dickey had the lowest ERA of any pitcher in the National League. His story is told in *Whenever I Wind Up.*

At one time Rick van Beek (from Byron Center, Michigan) smoked two packs of cigarettes a day. His daughter Madison has cerebral palsy, cannot speak, walk or see. She is thirteen years old but functions like a two-year-old. She inspired him to give up his smoking. He calls her "Maddy," and now Rick pulls her in a kayak when he swims; she sits in a cart when he bikes, and Rick pushes her in a stroller when he runs. He has become a triathlete. It has become a family affair. The other daughter Rachel also swims even though she is afraid of water, and Hunter, her brother, runs along side Rick. Beek admits that at times he thinks something seems impossible, but when he

28 Sojourners Silas House. *Singing the Stories Untold*, Vol 41, No 11, Dec. 2012, pp. 38-44

is tempted by despair or is momentarily not willing to pay the price, he looks at "Maddy" inside the cart laughing and smiling. The entire family admits that "Maddy" has made their whole lives better. The mother states that love enables them to reach out to "Maddy," and it is not finishing first that counts, but crossing the finish line.

JESUS' CALL TO CONVERT

While these stories are quite remarkable, Jesus requires more than a conversion *away* from something. His call is coupled with the demand that we also believe in the Gospel. Jesus' preaching was both a proclamation and a warning, a fundamental demand for a response. God takes the initiative and asks for our response. When we repent, we recognize and regret that we are "lost." We realize our hopeless situation in relationship to God and are willing to admit our sinfulness, as Peter did when "he fell at the knees of Jesus" and admitted he was a sinful man (Lk 5:8).

As noted, turning from a sinful way of living is only half the battle. Sin is often described as missing the mark, in Greek *harmartia*. Sin causes us to miss the mark because our lives are out of focus, disconnected from God. Relationships are severed; violence increases. In such a milieu, only a conversion to active, habitual compassion, peace, and forgiveness, can restore us to wholeness all of which are promised upon the vision that allows us to see everyone as created in God's image. Then we can receive each other despite our differences.

Turning *toward* Jesus or making a U-turn is even more challenging. This was true of Saul whose whole life was turned upside down by his encounter with Jesus. In his case we witness not simply a conversion, but an inversion. Saul, the great persecutor of the Church, now becomes a great convert, the Apostle to the Gentiles. His conversion and inversion were indeed costly, especially as he had to give up his position of prestige as a Pharisee, but he was willing to pay the price.

If we are asked, "Have you met Jesus?" some of us might respond, even if it is subconsciously, "unfortunately, yes." The conversion "jump" usually needs the help of a spiritual director, the support of another, or even a community. It is not easy to adopt the motto of John the Baptist, "He must increase and I must decrease," but it remains far more difficult to live that way (Jn 3:30). Reggie Jackson, who was known as Mr. October of baseball, once articulated such a process of decreasing can be when he said, "I have to deal with the magnitude of me." Some of us believe that conversion should happen immediately, that we should straightaway be free of all our imperfections or base inclinations. We might even have a timeline. We have instant coffee, tea, interest, information, and often expect instant spirituality. Conversion is multivalent, like a diamond with many sides. We need to be more patient and more open to the Spirit chastening our desires not to expect immediate results. We have to learn to calm down and be silent, to avoid the noisy rumblings around us so we can be attuned to how God is speaking to our innermost being. God's grace and mercy are not instant zaps. We need to be listened to with patience. Oftentimes God calls us to costly conversions that initially terrify us. Consider Daniel who was willing to live in a foreign land and whom God saved from the lions. Francis of Assisi risked being ridiculed by his own father, by his whole town. He was considered insane because of his actions, especially when he renounced his own father the social success laid out for him and lived a life of radical poverty.

The cost of conversion is brought out by Jesus when he says, "Whoever loves father or mother more than me, and whoever loves son or daughter more than me is not worthy of me" (Mt 10:37). He also exclaimed, "No one who sets a hand to the plow and looks to what was left behind is fit for the kingdom of God" (Lk 9:62). Those words are most challenging, and who of us is willing to pay the price of that kind of love or of letting go of everything to follow Jesus?

People asked John the Baptist what they ought to do to repent or convert. His reply was, "Whoever has two cloaks should share with the person who has none. And whoever has food should do likewise" (Lk 3:10-11). Justice should prompt and animate us to do this. The imbalance between those with less is rather obvious and needs to be addressed. Love will motivate us to be more attentive to their needs, and less concerned with defending our own interests. In his encyclical on love Pope Emeritus Benedict XVI states, "There will always be situations of material need where help in the form of concrete love of neighbor is indispensable."[29]

Just as love and justice are not opposed to one another, the sacraments of reconciliation and communion complete one another and give us what we need for conversion. In an address November 12, 2012, Cardinal Timothy Dolan of New York, president of the United States Conference of Catholic Bishops, challenged his brother bishops to their own conversion and renewal. He considers that the sacrament of reconciliation as the sacrament of the New Evangelization because it brings us in close contact with Jesus. But he also encouraged the Bishops to evangelize themselves first, before they attempt to transform society.

CONVERSION IS ONGOING

Conversion is an ongoing process, not a one shot deal or a flash occurrence. We can witness this in the prophets. Jeremiah complained and expressed his interior crisis, "O Lord, I let myself be duped...all the day I am an object of laughter; everyone mocks me" (20:7). He did not want to speak out, but a fire burning in his heart which enabled him to continue and not grow weary. After his initial "road to Damascus experience, Saul's conversion continued. He was invited to continue the process through inversion and immersion. Jesus told Ananias "I will show him what he will have to suffer for my name" (Acts 9:16).

---

[29] Benedict XVI, Pope. "Deus Caritas Est." http://www.vatican.va/holy_father/benedict_xvi/ encyclicals/documents/hf_ben-xvi_enc_20051225_deus-caritas-est_en.html. 5/18/13

Suffering is probably the most challenging part of *metanoia* because it is most costly, so costly that Paul enumerates all the intense suffering he endured for the sake of Christ in second Corinthians (11: 23-27). Are we willing to pay the price by accepting suffering in our lives?

Before leaving his Petrine ministry, Pope Emeritus Benedict XVI spoke about how difficult it is to live out one's faith in our modern society. He singled out Dorothy Day and her conversion. She confessed in her autobiography that she felt at one time that all things could be solved with politics. Dorothy moved away from her faith for years only to discover Christ and his Gospel in a new way, seeing for the first time that the Catholic Church was "the church of the poor." Her prayer life and ongoing conversion enabled her to dedicate herself to the underprivileged. Benedict XVI also spoke of Etty Hillesum, a Dutch Jewish woman, who died in Auschwitz. Initially, she was far from God, but gradually, as she described her trial in words, found God deep within the well of her goodness. Etty wrote in her diary that most times she could reach God, but at other times God seemed buried and she needed to dig up God again. Despite the turmoil in which she lived, her faith and ongoing conversion helped her to live in constant intimacy with God.

The task of ongoing conversion is daunting. We are faced with many threatening crises in our world which can easily overwhelm us. This is especially true of violence and fear. They are "whale" size as Judy Cannato, a retreat facilitator, states. We can easily become paralyzed by their enormity. Our natural impulse is to run or flee because of fear. We need to make a U turn in our lives if are to help our culture survive. We cannot depend on some detached deity or outside force to save us. Rather, we must first look to ourselves. It will require all our capabilities, all our freedom, all our love and compassion. The cost will entail our willingness to die with Christ, to immerse ourselves into his paschal mystery so we can rise with him in new life. And share that life with others.

Jesus challenged us to "Produce good fruit as evidence of your repentance" (Mt. 3:8). The questions we need to ask are *Am I teachable? Do I welcome correction?* We read in Proverbs, "Reprove a wise man, and he will love you; instruct a wise man, and he becomes still wiser; teach a just man, and he advances in learning" (9:8-9). We know the Spirit is alive in us, we can discern the Spirit's presence if we "Belong to God, and anyone who knows God listens to us, while anyone who does not belong to God refuses to hear us. This is how we know the spirit of truth and the spirit of deceit" (I Jn 4:6).

NEEDED IN MARRIAGE

Ongoing conversion is especially necessary in marriage. Many marriages become miserable because of a perceived incompatibility, because of resentment that arises from differences. The rift can be financial, emotional, social, or sexual in origin. In contrast, spouses of healthy marriages treasure their differences. Difference can be a source of delight. Once differences become threatening, problems will arise and many spouses are not willing to pay the price of solving them. The challenge is to allow the differences to become an adventure, not a dead end street. Often widowed spouses regret that they did not affirm the good qualities of each other while he or she was alive. Valuing differences, however, does not entail putting up with alcoholism, drugs, pornography, infidelity, verbal and physical abuse. These last things are justice issues which need to be confronted, and at times professional advice might be needed.

Brent Barlow, a family counselor, maintains that if spouses want to improve their marriages they should look into a mirror, as one tends to blame the partner when the deeper problem might be oneself. We react to some stimuli like verbal abuse or a cutting remark in a similar fashion. Too often the spouse will say, "He/she makes me so mad." "He/she is so lazy." Either spouse becomes a victim, so someone is good and the other bad, which leads to more resentment, anger and impatience. Howard Markman, a psychologist, examined couples while they were in heated arguments. He found they fall into three categories: "those who digress into threats and name calling, those who revert to silent fuming, and those who speak openly, honestly and effectively."[30] The longer it takes for spouses to resume speaking to each other, the harder it becomes and the higher the costs.

---

[30] Patterson, Kerry. Joseph Grenny, Ron McMillan, and Al Switzler. *Crucial Conversations*, pp 14-15

The story is told of spouses who were giving each the silent treatment after a heated argument. After some days the husband realized that he needed his wife to wake him up for an early fishing trip. But he did not want to be the first to break the silence, so he wrote her a note which read, "Please wake me up at 5 A.M.," and put it by her pillow. The following morning he woke up and it was 7 A.M. and he missed his trip. He was about to angrily tell her off, when he noticed a slip of paper next to his pillow. It read, "It's 5 A.M. Wake up!" Quite a wake up call!

The price of ongoing conversion entails that spouses respond to harsh words with kind words. They are given the choice and they become their choices. Jesus said, "When someone strikes you your right cheek, turn the other one as well" (Mt. 5:39). That is most challenging, so most of us simply discard it and settle for more pragmatic means. Rather than being offended by a cranky spouse who has experienced a hard day, try being considerate and understanding. Another good way to respond to some offensive remark is developing a sense of humor. Humor contains the surprise element and it can cut through the tension much like a knife cutting through a pad of butter. Oftentimes humor is a fruit of conversion. Oliver Wendell Holmes was invited to a party and he happened to be the smallest person present. A friend said to him, "I should think you would feel rather small amongst us big fellows." "I do," he retorted, "I feel like a dime among pennies."

Often conflicts in marriage stem from the fact that one spouse attacks the other's self-worth. Spouses become aggressive when they feel inadequate, unloved, rejected or devalued. Stephen Covey portrays this as an "identity theft." He considers the aggressive spouse's actions cruel. A spouse might say, "Why can't you be as industrious as your brother," or "Why can't you clean the house like your sister?" One's self-worth becomes as fragile as a snow flake or a spider's web, especially if one's value hinges largely on the spouse's estimation.

Spouses can suddenly become aware that their partner is not making the other miserable, but that he/she is. This is part of the conversion process. They need to remember that no one can hurt them—except in cases of abuse—unless they allow the spouse to do it. Spouses can make a decision that will determine how they are going to respond. Too often they respond in anger or repress the feeling. Ignoring the problem will not make it go away. What they resist will persist. Spouses dislike doing this, but if the marriage is to grow stronger, this is absolutely necessary. Oftentimes we over-dramatize the cost of tackling problems directly. George Herbert, an English poet, maintained that good words are worth much and cost so very little.

The amazing part is that some spouses have the ability not to be offended or shamed. They cannot prevent their spouse from saying something offensive, but they can control their response. The hardest part is preventing the anger, resentment, or hurt from controlling them, and, in turn, transforming it into something good for the sake of the marriage. At the outset of marriage, spouses are wired to act the way they do. To rewire their brain demands practice and much discipline to move from aggressive reaction to compassion and allow the ongoing process of conversion to continue.

The irony is that in many dysfunctional relationships the very qualities that attracted them to each other often become the qualities which cause coldness, indifference and dislike. Maybe the best advice to spouses is, "Don't try to make each other better, but make each other happier." Don't try to remake them according to your image and likeness, but respect their unique gifts rather than their differences, or else their "conversion" will be away from God and toward you. Knowing your spouse's heart will enable you to move beyond what divides them.

Some spouses live for years in "emotional divorce" because they continue to argue over the same issues, especially money. Diverse values, behavior and beliefs can be assimilated into a new approach. Through many difficult conversations and changes, some mediated by professionals or third parties, *my* way becomes *our* way, which brings new life, the result of conversion. In a Christian sense, *wanting* change or ongoing conversion involves the head, *willing* it the heart, and *doing* it the gut. All three are necessary if we are to open ourselves to conversion, to accept the inversion or the turning, the *metanoia* of our lives. By far the most challenging part of the process is the immersion into Jesus Christ's mystery of suffering. And yet, as is most evident in marriage but likewise true of any state of life, suffering well leads us closer to salvation.

SCRIPTURE PASSAGES FOR REFLECTION

"For my thoughts are not your thoughts, nor your ways my ways."
>(Is 55:8)

"For God all things are possible."
>(Mt 19:26)

"Without vision the people perish."
>(Prov 29:18)

"Repent, and believe in the Gospel."
>(Mk 1:15).

"Whoever loves mother or father more than me, and whoever loves son or daughter more than me is not worthy of me."
>(Mt 10:37)

QUESTIONS TO CONSIDER

1. Do you procrastinate in what needs to be done?
2. Do you resist change, and if so, why?
3. Have you experienced a conversion, or know of someone who has?
4. Why is immersion into Jesus the most difficult part of conversion?
5. Why is the task of ongoing conversion so daunting especially in marriage?

111

CHAPTER SIX
THE COST OF SUFFERING

The age old question continues to haunt us: *why
do bad things happen to good people, and good things
happen to bad people?* None of us can claim we are
righteous. Only Jesus and Mary were righteous, yet even
they suffered. When we consider this, on what grounds
can we claim that goodness or a life filled with good deeds
should be freed from trials? Maybe the harder question
should be, *why do we consider some people "good,"* when
no one is really good?

Solomon wrestled with the idea of why bad things
occur to good people and good things occur to bad people.
Surveying human existence he said, "I have seen all
manner of things in my vain days: a just man perishing in
his justice, and a wicked one surviving in his wickedness"
(Eccl 9:15). With all of his wisdom he could not
understand this age old question either. Job also had to
grapple with this problem. We have to keep in mind while
reading Job that many of Job's contemporaries, Jewish and
otherwise, believed if they led a good life here on earth
God would reward them. If they led an evil life, so the
theology went, they were already punished. According to
this thought process, then, evidently Job did something

wrong. Some of his closest friends gave him advice, but the wrong kind. Many of these friends claimed to be experts. We can think of Bernard Murdock, supposed top-man of his profession, giving twisted advice to so many people. Even Job's wife told him to curse God. But he responded, "Naked I came forth from my mother's womb, and naked shall I go back again. The Lord gave and the Lord has taken away; blessed be the name of the Lord" (1:21)!

Suffering can be very perplexing, confusing, upsetting, and often causes anger. Trying to figure it out is like putting together a 500-piece jigsaw puzzle or bucket full of Rubik's cubes. The impulse to ask *why* we suffer can be as annoying as a mosquito buzzing around at night in one's room; as strong as the sense that some answer exists, somewhere, that answer eludes us—especially when we experience the loss of a loved one.

The encounter with mortality, be it our own or someone else's, is a major force that gives rise to such questions. Elderly people agonize about going to a nursing home, often interpreting it as the beginning of the end. I have witnessed much suffering while visiting them. One man told me, "Don't get old, Father." My response was, "What is the other option?" Another one cried out, "It's hell getting old." Getting old *is* filled with all sorts of unexpected and even bizarre symptoms and struggles. I am reminded of our former President George Bush who visited a nursing home and asked one of the residents, "Do you know who I am?" The resident responded, "No, but if you go to the nurse's desk, they might be able to tell you." The suffering that comes with old age takes many forms, including mental confusion, dementia, memory loss. Each of these is like a little death.

Despite all the technological advancements we have made, especially in terms of artificial hearts, pacemakers, bionic eyes, robots, we still have not found the cure for the common cold. I remember reading about a company that was determined to find the cure, but after many, many, experiments they finally gave up. No sound bites or magic pills will alleviate all suffering.

In light of this, the crucial question remains, *is there a purpose in suffering*? We are pilgrims here on earth and dark valleys of suffering cover our paths. We have not yet reached Mount Tabor, where we would like to stay as Peter did free from all suffering. St. Paul suffered more than any Apostle, and it is to him we can first turn to seek the *purpose* of suffering. To the Church in Rome he wrote: "I consider the sufferings of the present time are as nothing compared with the glory to be revealed for us" (Rom 8:18). He wanted "To know him and the power of his resurrection and the sharing of his sufferings by being conformed to his death" (Phil 3:10). Like Paul I have done some traveling around the country—admittedly not usually by boat—and have come in contact with people who suffer intensely. I met a man who had thirteen operations in one year. Among his other trials, he contracted cancer of the tongue, which had to be removed. After I spoke we carried on our conversation. How? He wrote something on a piece of paper. I'll never forget what he wrote: "Father, we will do anything to keep alive." He reminded me of Zechariah, father of John the Baptist, who doubted that his wife could become pregnant and was struck speechless. I also came in contact with a woman who had thirteen miscarriages. What amazed me about her was that she was not resentful or angry. Another lady whom I visited had both her legs amputated. I can still picture her sitting on her sofa smiling and asking me how the mission was going. My intention was to cheer up these people, but *I was truly inspired by them.* Suffering produces a wisdom that one cannot receive without it.

Some people resist or try to flee from *all* suffering, which can be as disastrous as driving with your emergency brake on. In trying to rid ourselves of all suffering we compound the suffering even more. We often increase our suffering due to dysfunctional, untrue and erroneous beliefs that we can rid ourselves of it. We can correct our own unhealthy attitudes toward suffering by visiting loved ones in nursing homes, loved ones we might rather avoid because they have Alzheimer or dementia. Certainly this is difficult to bear. But so was the cross. And surely we'd rather be Mary or John, at the foot of the cross, than the scattered, fearful disciples, who disappeared at Christ's darkest hour. A man whose wife had Alzheimer's and visited her every day was asked, "Why do that, when she doesn't even know who you are?" He responded, "She might not know who I am, but I know who she is." The possibility of redemptive suffering is foreign to most people today, even though it was a way of life in the early Church. Is the price of suffering too high for us to accept?

So, if suffering is part and parcel of our lives, why does it shock us? We can get so caught up on why God allows it that we begin to doubt God's existence. Even if we have a Rolodex for a brain, we will never be able to resolve the mystery of suffering. In his book *Be A Man* Father Larry Richards uses the example of a son who is afraid of needles in order to get at the heart of suffering. He contracts pneumonia and needs a shot. The father holds his fearful son while the shot is given, knowing that he feels betrayed by his father. The father, however, has to assure him that this shot will cure him. Suffering can also cause us to become fearful. God, however, is there as a loving God in the face of unresolved questions concerning suffering. Who knows what is best for us, God or ourselves? Are we willing to pay the price of believing in a loving God?

God can use suffering to help refine, perfect and strengthen us. It can teach us humility so we can acquire the mind of Christ. Peter encourages us, "So, humble yourselves under the mighty hand of God, that he may exalt you in due time. Cast all your worries upon him because he cares for you" (I Pt 5:6-7). The Lord is more concerned about our character than our comfort. We can learn obedience and self control through suffering in a manner we simply could not without it. Of Jesus' suffering the book of Hebrews tells us, "Because he himself was tested through what he suffered, he is able to help those who are being tested" (2:18). Also, "Son though he was, he learned obedience from what he suffered" (5:8). Jesus can identify with our suffering and invites us, "Come to me, all you who labor and are burdened, and I will give you rest" (Mt 11:30).

JESUS GIVES SUFFERING MEANING

We need to see suffering in relationship to Jesus, because *he, and ultimately he alone,* gives it meaning. Our world is filled with violence, injustice, idolatry and immorality, but Jesus overcomes all this by his suffering and death. Isaiah pointed this out when he spoke about him as the suffering servant, "Not crying, not shouting, not making his voice heard in the street. A bruised reed he shall not break and a smoldering wick he shall not quench, until he establishes justice on the earth" (42: 2-4). Jesus responds to the world's suffering in a peaceful, gentle way, not in an arrogant, brutal manner. He will do it in a *new* way. This is Jesus' job description. He calls us to set things right by *not* pretending we know all the answers to complicated problems, by *not* using violent displays to accomplish our goals. We need to walk with people in pain and suffering, praying for and with them, bringing hope to the hopeless. This challenge can be costly, but it is another price we as Christians must pay.

The cross is the linchpin of history because all evil and pain combine in one person, in one place. What Jesus accomplished there becomes the final act of love rather than an outright scandal. All Jesus' words and many miracles of mercy meet in a death embrace that gave us new life and hope. All the joys of Easter are filtered through the prism of the cross. The cross is the clearest window through which we can understand who Jesus is, the suffering servant, who helps us to bear our cross. The broken and suffering servant Jesus makes us whole. We bring our sorrows of loved ones who died, people who are unemployed, homes destroyed by hurricanes and floods, and fold them into Jesus' passion. Jesus wept at the grave of Lazarus, and shares our griefs. And carries our sorrows.

SUFFERING SERVANT

The so called "suffering servant" in Isaiah 49 feels that he has toiled in vain, but then realizes his reward is from God. This passage points out that God will accomplish the rescue not only of Israel but of the whole world. Don't we at times feel that things have gone down the tube? Aren't we wasting our time trying to decrease poverty, hunger, drugs, racism and many other societal ills? Here again we find hope in the example of Jesus who died on the cross and was considered by many a failure, a disgrace. But the Father raised him, and Jesus declared, "Now the ruler of this world will be driven out. And when I am lifted up from the earth, I will draw everyone to myself" (Jn 12:31-32). We can now claim victory over evil powers such as misery, despair, and hopelessness, because of Jesus' suffering and death on the cross. He paid the price for us, so that even if we *feel* that the scales are tipping in the wrong direction, in truth, in fact, the scale is always tipped toward salvation.

118

Many of the sins committed today are found in the story of Jesus' suffering and passion: lying committed by false witnesses; injustice done by the rich against the weak, poor, and oppressed; idolatry of military might; love of power as shown by Caiaphas; and finally, betrayal. We know how we react if we have been betrayed, lied to, treated unjustly. The blame game is rampant in our society. Do we hang on to our hurts, blame others, or take the high moral road? We become our choices. Jesus suffered and died to show us his great love. The suffering servant in Isaiah is depicted as one who "gave my back to those who beat me...my face I did not shield from buffets and spitting." But God is with him, "The Lord God is my help, therefore I am not disgraced" (50:6-7). He absorbs all the evil, like a sponge, trusting that God will vindicate him. We need to bring all the bad things that have happened to us, or any unkindness that we might have done to others, to the foot of the cross. Jesus will forgive us and he asks us to forgive others and ourselves. Are we willing to pay the price of forgiveness? We can hardly countenance suffering without doing so.

Good Friday did not make much sense to many, because they put all their faith in Jesus as a different sort of messiah than he actually was, only to see his life snuffed out. Had Satan tricked them again like Eve and Adam? Maybe there was no God at all. Anyone's faith would be tested by witnessing Jesus being scourged, beaten, mocked and tortured beyond one's imagination. Nothing but darkness, violence, earthquakes, pierced the air at his death. This is brought out forcefully by the last of Haydn's seven sonatas, as its final movement represents the earthquake. How can calm replace chaos, and hope overcome fear? We live in much fear. I remember as a kid that we did not lock our house, and we were not afraid to walk the streets even at night. We knew everyone in our neighborhood and beyond. That is certainly not true today because we are fearful of the violence surrounding us.

We read in Isaiah: "He was spurned and avoided by men, a man of suffering, accustomed to infirmity. One of those from whom men hide their faces, spurned, and we held him in no esteem. Yet it was our infirmities he bore, our sufferings he endured" (53:3-4). We have in this passage a graphic picture of injustices and oppression, and people getting away with it. Jesus did for us what we could not do for ourselves. A spirit of gratitude needs to flood our hearts. Yet the sort of battle Jesus embodies is more profound than David fighting Goliath, because Christ conquered *all* death and chaos for our sake. When Jesus cried out, "It is finished," the words sum up his whole life lived for us. This meant the bill had been paid in full. He was willing to pay the price of his shedding his last drop of blood. Those closest to Jesus, Mary and John experienced dramatic life changes. Have *our* lives changed when we've reflected on or even mystically *felt* the intensity of his own suffering and death? Can we stand at the foot of the cross and allow Jesus to speak to us words of encouragement in our suffering? If we don't find consolation at the foot of the cross, where will we find it? Only when we understand the true meaning of the cross, are we able to bring our basket full of sorrows, disappointments, setbacks, and lay them at the foot of the cross.

WAITING AND SUFFERING

The process of suffering unfolds something like a potter making piece of pottery. The potter picks up the clay, adds drops of water to make it more flexible and easier to work with. He has to wait until the correct texture is acquired and then lifts it high to let it drop. Plop! That motion removes all the air bubbles and flaws, a process that can symbolize how our imperfections are gradually removed. Next, the clay is put on the wheel and shaped exactly as the potter wants. Then he places the clay in the kiln to be fired. The clay might wonder why it is so hot, but this is the price the clay has to endure. The potter has to wait until the right time before removing the pottery and letting it cool. Then he glazes the pottery to make it even more beautiful. Suffering, even though costly, can do the same for us.

Suffering involves waiting to see how things will turn out. The book Lamentations expressed this waiting period well, "Come, all you who pass by the way, look and see whether there is any suffering like my suffering which has been dealt me" (1:12). Yes, waiting and being patient often does not make sense, just as our suffering often does not make sense, and we often feel the need to talk about our suffering to others. But under the weight of many crosses, it takes much faith to see that there is purpose and meaning in the chaos and the ruin. When everything seems utterly meaningless, hope has to emerge into something new. But our hope dims, as it did for the disciples, who said on the way to Emmaus, "We were hoping that he would be the one to redeem Israel" (Lk 24:21). The living water, the good shepherd, the manna come down from heaven, the light of the world, the light of the nations has fallen silent. Can we wait and live in the silence of our suffering? We need to wait as we bring our sufferings to the cross and see what God will do. We also have to face and embrace our anger, grief and sorrow as we wait in the tomb so that something new can arise.

A boy has to wait to grow in manhood before he more readily understands how something good can come of suffering. Much suffering results from growing old gracefully, as this gracefulness is a waiting process. Dustin Hoffman, who is over seventy years old, considers it thrilling to hold a paintbrush because of what he can accomplish with it. He now directs movies, and remembers Bill Connolly, one of the stars of Quartet, saying, "Don't die until you're dead." As our bodies decline, our souls should expand. Manoel de Oliveira is directing movies at 104. A ninety-four-year-old man ran a triathlon. Asked if he was going to run again, he responded, "Oh, yeah, I got to keep going till I get older."

But others are not as spry or energetic, but are troubled with arthritis, rheumatism, or other aches and pains that accompany old age. The challenge is to accept the suffering, unite it all to Jesus' suffering, and look forward with hope to the rich reward God has in store for them in the next life.

Jesus had to wait in the tomb until the silence was broken on Easter. We experience forty days of Lent. Why not experience forty days of partying because Jesus has truly risen? How can Easter give us fresh hope in our suffering? I would say that we first need to ask where Jesus was after he died. To the good thief he said, "Today you will be with me in Paradise" (Lk 23:43). In *Christians at the Cross* Bishop N.T. Wright shows that paradise is not our final destination. The book of Revelation speaks of a new heaven and a new earth (21:1). In other words, everything that is bad or sad will be changed or abolished. We will be raised up and given a new body, which will enable us to live in a new world, one we cannot fully imagine. We already possess some taste of this, as we wait in the "already and the not yet," a Christian mystery, but we need to live in relation to the new heaven and new earth, so that we don't fall into the habit of seeing *this* earth as the end all.

I remember calling Australia on the feast of All Saints in connection with my forthcoming trip there. The friar who answered gave me an All Souls Day greeting. They are one day ahead of us. We, in a sense, are on old time. But suddenly realizing that, metaphorically, the Australian friar was ahead of me, living in God's new world a day ahead of me; this might support us in our efforts to embrace our suffering. Are we willing—because we have witnessed the worst happening to Jesus, who destroyed death, sin and gives us new life—to face the future with an evergreen hope burning in our hearts? From this disposition, from this vantage point, our mission is to help this new creation come more alive in our society. To accomplish this task we need to leave our suffering, trials, difficulties, and heartaches at the cross instead of complaining about them. The resurrection helps us to find new possibilities as we renew our baptismal commitment on Easter. So we put our shoulders to the wheel of possibilities.

Both Augustine and Thomas Aquinas maintain that God allows evil or suffering to bring about a greater good. They consider this as part of God's providential plan. But, we might ask, how can any good come from the Holocaust or the killing of innocent people in war, or the death of a three year old child? All of these and similar incidents are connected with suffering which often seems pointless. Perhaps we can recall Simone Weil's distinction between arbitrary suffering and redemptive suffering. Whereas some suffering is simply awful, almost entirely fruitless, purely the result of sin and disorder, other suffering can contribute to our mystical work of evangelizing the world.

We no longer simply have pietas carved out of marble and stone. Now we have them in the suffering widows of Syria and other countries. Consider the countless refugees who are dying where they hoped to live. When suffering fails to move us, we may have reached an unhealthy state of disconnect. We are disconnected from God and others. Sufferings can bond us together into a common purpose. John, now prisoner on the island of Patmos wrote, "I, John, your brother, who share with you the distress, the kingdom, and the endurance we have in Jesus" (Rev 1:9). St. Paul insisted "If one member suffers, all members suffer" (I Cor 12:26). God encourages us "in our every affliction, so we may be able to encourage those who are in any affliction with the encouragement with which we ourselves are encouraged by God" (2 Cor 1:4). "For this momentary light affliction is producing for us an eternal weight of glory beyond all comparison" (2 Cor 4:17). "I consider that the sufferings of this present time are as nothing compared with the glory to be revealed for us" (Rom 8:18). Are we willing to be hope-filled people who pay the price of realizing and carrying out these powerful and uplifting words of St. Paul?

Some people are not very hope-filled but, rather, have a tendency to blame God for their suffering. God becomes the scapegoat, especially when earthquakes, floods, tornadoes, and hurricanes cause so much havoc. These can be attributed to natural causes. We are not pawns on the human chessboard of life. God is not a cruel master, in spite of what many think. The problem of "blaming God" was brought out to me when I visited a father and his two sons. The mother died of cancer at the age of forty-two. The father lashed out at God and said, 'How could God do this to us?" As a result, he decided that he and his sons would discontinue their church going. Under trying circumstances like these, we are given a choice to become a bitter or a better person, a hardened or a softer individual. Again, the price we pay to become better or softer is high.

Are we willing to pay the price of allowing suffering to transform our lives? Solzhenitsyn believed that people of Russia are more spiritual than those living in the West because they suffered more. Maybe we have to fall apart and hit bottom before we grow. That was evident in the case of the prodigal son and is true of many alcoholics. Mother Teresa's spiritual director told her that one of the reasons she had to suffer spiritual aridity in prayer, and to feel like she was in hell, was because that enabled her to identify more with the poor. Yet, she paid the price of being a joy-filled person and insisted that her followers do the same.

JOY IN SUFFERING

Paul found joy in his own suffering when he wrote "Now I rejoice in my suffering" (Col 1:24). Who in their right mind would rejoice in their suffering? Someone taking pleasure in their pain might. Maybe you have met some people who are not happy unless they are miserable. Their misery gives them contentment, which makes for a distorted view of life. What a contrast to a lady I read about who living in Clearwater, Florida, at the age of 113 looked outside and seeing it was raining, said, "That's okay, we'll make our own sunshine." This is similar to what Paul means when he says he *rejoices* in suffering. He is not masochistic, but, rather, can maintain great joy amidst his trials.

126

Jesus pronounced a blessing on those "who are persecuted for the sake of righteousness or when they insult you and utter every kind of evil against you (falsely) because of me" (Mt 5:10-12) Jesus looked upon suffering accepted *in* Christ, not suffering *in itself*, as a way to unite ourselves more intimately to him. He invites us, through trials, to become more like him. After the Apostles were flogged by the Sanhedrin for teaching in the temple, they rejoiced because they were found worthy to suffer for Christ's sake (Acts 5:41). Paul could even boast about his afflictions because suffering "produces endurance. and endurance proven character, and proven character hope, and hope does not disappoint" (Rom 5:3-5). For Paul, affliction is a means by which we can develop a healthy Christian character based on hope. And hope does not disappoint us.

At the Last Supper Jesus assured his Apostles, "I say to you, you will weep and mourn, while the world rejoices, you will grieve, but your grief will become joy" (Jn 16:20). He also gave the example of a woman in labor and her pain, followed by the tremendous joy of giving birth to a child. The image of childbirth is used in the Hebrew Scriptures in reference to God's actions, especially to God's decisive future act of salvation. Turning a catastrophe into a joyous event is an important part of the Gospel story. When we are put in the cellars of pain and suffering, we need to remember that God keeps the best wine there, not in the open sunshine where wine cannot fully ferment. We find some of the best pearls in deep waters. We do not have to be happy all the time. Some people give that impression, but they might be hurting just as we are. In a culture that has lost its ability to make important distinctions, it is worth emphasizing that *joy* is different from *happiness*. Whereas happiness is happenstance, joy is calmer, less emotional. More real.

Michael Fox has lived with Parkinson's disease for two decades, but still can be joyful. His hands tremble, his right knee swings, his shoulders shake up and down, but he does not like to be pitied. Rather, he jokes, saying, "Who needs an electronic toothbrush when you have a vibrating hand?" Fox is sure to note that simply because he shaves with a razor one should not consider him suicidal. Pouring cereal, he doesn't know what is going to happen; the bran flakes can be all over the floor. Even when his mind tells him to stop clapping, he keeps on going. Fox believes his disease is a gift that has brought him closer to his wife Pollan of 25 years.[31]

Many of us realize that as we grow older we have matured as persons through, not in spite of, our suffering. At crucial moments of pain we made choices to become bitter or better, sad or joyful. We can become an ecosystem bent on producing toxic dysfunction or an ecosystem bent on producing joy. The aim is not to *always* be happy, but to move toward joy. Paul was given that choice while in jail; he could have become sad and dismal. Instead he encouraged the Philippians "Rejoice in the Lord always. I

---

[31] For more information, consult *AARP* Vol. 56, No2, April, May, 2013, pp. 38-41.

shall say it again, rejoice" (4:4). No hint of complaining or feeling sorry for himself was evident, but rather he emboldened others in their suffering. Rejoicing in our suffering does not mean being stoical, keeping a stiff upper lip, toughing it out, hanging in there, grinning and bearing it. Non-Christians can do that and put us to shame by what they endure. It is most challenging to accept suffering *as an experience of God's love* for us as Paul did. Of course, often the opposite is true; we feel rejected, broken, worthless when we are hurting. At those times we need to embrace the cross of Jesus who showed us how much he loved us by dying on it. He was willing to pay suffering's highest price—the price of his life—for us.

I'll never forget a woman I visited in the Detroit area who was suffering from rheumatoid arthritis in her hands. It was so bad that she could not even hold a telephone. In the course of our conversation she said, "I thank God for my suffering." What a tremendous grace that is! How many of us, even when we do something as simple and annoying as burning the toast, could say, "Thank you Lord?" Or, let's say we cannot get our car started on a cold morning: who could utter, "Thank you, Lord." Usually we get upset and angry. It is amazing what can happen if we learn to thank God even when things go wrong. While giving a renewal during winter on the south side of Milwaukee, I remember stepping outside the rectory early in the morning. Not knowing there was some black ice there, I fell flat on my back. I do not recall saying, "Thank you, Lord." Nevertheless, in similar situations I keep remembering this lady and her attitude toward suffering.

Hope enables us to look beyond this life to the reward that God has in store for us in heaven. That might explain why many saints who suffered so much did so joyfully. So we rejoice in our sufferings because when Christ comes in glory, we will rejoice with him forever.

Yes, the wisdom of suffering is shrouded in mystery. Mystery, however, is not some dark secret or something distant and aloof like a Howard Hughes. Rather it implies a richness, a depth and breadth difficult to grasp. It is a mystery to be lived and not solved. The price we pay is living the mystery. Suffering is like a piece of tapestry. One side of the cloth is a mass of mix up colors, bumps and knots. This is the side that we keep looking at as we make our journey through life, a sight which causes much confusion, doubt and anxiety. Our earth is awash with so many fears, trials and tragedies. But some day we will see the beautiful pattern our lives have woven when the opposite side appears. The beauty will be embroidered and in direct proportion to how we have embraced suffering in our lives or the lives of loved ones. We will understand how our hardships, difficulties, doubts and setbacks have crisscrossed with Jesus' life as it is Christ who will reveal to us the meaning of suffering, especially the meaning behind the injustices we all experience.

SCRIPTURE PASSAGES FOR REFLECTION

"If anyone wishes to come after me, he must deny himself and take up his cross and follow me."

(Lk 9:23)

"Son though he was, he learned obedience from what he suffered."

(Heb 5:8)

"Come to me, all you who labor and are burdened, and I will give you rest."

(Mt 11:30)

"If one member suffers, all members suffer."

(I Cor 12:26)

"I consider the sufferings of the present time are as nothing compared with the glory to be revealed for us."

(Rom 8:18)

"Now I rejoice in my sufferings."

(Col 1:24)

QUESTIONS TO CONSIDER

1. How do you react to your own suffering, or to a loved one's suffering?
2. Do you question the purpose of suffering?
3. How has Jesus' suffering helped you to bear your own?
4. How can you reach out to others who are suffering?
5. How can you be joyful in your suffering?
6. How does Christ's resurrection give you hope in your suffering?

CHAPTER SEVEN
COSTLY JUSTICE ISSUES

Since it is impossible to consider all the so called "justice issues," I have singled out a few which demand that advocates pay the price. Opposing injustice is comparable to walking through a minefield blindfolded. Justice issues are deeply imbedded, are seemingly everywhere, making our response to them very challenging. Too many poor have been put under the boot of oppression. Pope Francis believes that—in addition to their being condemnable from a Christian perspective—terrorism, repression, murder, human trafficking, violate human and basic *rights*. Unfortunate events happen in our lives which we are often unable to control such as the Boston Marathon. The task to rehumanize, which is part of the process of justice, people we have dehumanized can be costly, but this needs to be done.

One of our most serious challenges today is how to stop terrorism, which interrupts the safety and often the sanity of people's lives. Instead of merely placing checkpoints at various places, why not have welcoming signs as our bags are checked?

Costly attempts to close the gap between the rich and the poor can challenge our justice system. Scores of people are not able to pay their monthly mortgages while others are feeding their families with food stamps. Many unions have deunionized themselves, anti-labor forces have deunionized workers, increased the number of unemployed and welfare recipients, and former soldiers and prisoners are begging for jobs. Are they living what is some times called "the broken promise of American democracy"? Most of them are civic, spirited and patriotic. But are they engaged in a game where they are bound to lose? The plight of the poor, the homeless, the jobless and those addicted to drugs can easily overwhelm us. We often salve our conscience by making a small donation or an act of kindness, but easily then forget about them. For Simone Weil, when we treat our afflicted neighbors with love we are, in a sense, baptizing them. Refraining from purchasing the latest gadget or fasting one day a week these things might enable us to work against our consumerist lifestyle.[32] In the spirit of his namesake, Pope Francis has criticized consumerism and urged us to live a simple life style. He encouraged us not to wash our hands of injustices that we face but to assume responsibility, to do something to surmount them. One couple did this in the following manner. Now that their children are grown, they have simplified their lives by giving up their car and using public transportation or renting a car. They admitted that not seeing their friends as often or easily was challenging, but they were willing to pay the price. Many couples at

[32] Kathryn, Hermes FSP. *Beginning Contemplative Prayer*. Cincinnati, OH; St. Anthony Messenger, 2001, p. 94.

this stage in their lives would purchase a fancy car, do some luxury traveling, and live it up. But this couple wanted to live simply so that others might live. This is a superb example that many can imitate if they are willing to pay the price. Their voluntary poverty has drawn them closer to God, to each other, and to every *other*.

Once we discover our own potential, we find that we are not as limited in our choices as we often believe we are. Too many of us wait for destiny to knock on our doors. Helping people to think in terms of what they *can* contribute to society will enable them to possess a healthy, spiritually-nourished outlook on life. All of us are of infinite worth, no matter how poor we are. To realize our worth, we have to overcome our fear of failure, rejection, and other things that can easily lead to despair. We hear people say, "Why don't the poor get a job?" And yet, as I know from my own experience of living among the poor for many years, most don't have connections, education, and good health, all of which prevents them from accepting this overwhelming challenge. We don't solve the problem by handing out more food stamps and ferverinos. Consider the complexity of even the simplest changes for the poorest of the poor. A mother could take her obese child to the doctor, and he says that the child needs a healthier diet and lots of exercise. When she returns to her community, it lacks a farmer's market, no full-service grocery stores: all she encounters are corner stores that sell potato chips, soda and liquor. Engaging in the war on poverty is daunting, and who of us are willing to pay the price?

We live in a warped and twisted world which needs redemption. Too many people have a defeatist attitude. Too many pessimistically assume that we cannot adequately tackle poverty, hunger, racism or our national debt. We are not a poor country; some of the wealthiest and most capable people in the world live in the United States, so the question is not whether we *can,* but whether we *will* respond to the needs of the poor. What choices are we going to make to build a better future? What we need is a holistic approach to serving those in need wherein we support them not just materially, but mentally, emotionally and (especially) spiritually. The journey out of poverty is a long and arduous one. Many of our poor have become jaded, ridden with depression or even despair. Ralph Waldo Emerson wrote that we become what we think about most all day long. Tasks that others ordinarily accomplish quite easily can, for many poor people, require much energy. Once they find a job, the next challenge is to keep it.

The most effective way to rid our world of poverty is from the inside out. In many instances people have to learn to help themselves rather than depend on outside help. They need to see themselves as gifted and able to solve their problems. The Westboro Baptist Church of Topeka, Kansas, has a saying, "The arm of God cannot be shortened." This means we cannot do anything to make God do less than God will do; we cannot lessen God's ability to save. When we apply this saying to others, we realize we cannot limit or shorten their potential to be loved by God, to be people of love.[33] At times, the answers to poverty come from unexpected places, proving that God's hand will reach where it wills. Some of the most profound answers originate among the poorest of the poor. India has found out that many of their country's problems can be solved not necessarily in the universities, but via innovative ways by which the poor can utilize their own gifts. Students from the Indian Institute of Management at Ahmedabad go to the countryside for eight to ten days. They look for creative ideas used by farmers and shop workers which they can bring back and share with others.[34] This is a superb example, and we would do well to borrow its spirit and sensibility, and applying it elsewhere.

UNITED FRONT

In order to achieve justice in a pluralistic world, we need to change the "us" and "them," and not inculcate a win-lose solution, so that Muslims, Christians, Jews can live together, working *together,* at the very least for mutual material welfare. Tribal solidarities, racism, bigotry, and intolerance result in enmity, violence, and backlash. Unity in our efforts will insure the importance of planting our feet firmly on the ground. Dr. Rabbi Ron Kornish, director of Interreligious Coordinating Council in Israel based in Jerusalem, observes that Israelis and Palestinians seldom meet with each other during the day. Instead, each side is

---

[33] Joanie, Eppinga. "The Face of Hate," *Sojourners.* Vol 41, No 6, June 2012, p. 18.

[34] Stephen, Covey. *The 3ʳᵈ Alternative.* New York, NY; Free Press, 2011, p. 364.

told how terrible the other side is, often from a very young age. Opportunities for them to get together and dialogue are in short supply. Only this can change their hearts and minds. By studying each others' sacred texts, they can develop a level of trust, openness and build bridges. They can engage in reality instead of ideology. One reason why diplomatic efforts often fail is that they don't meet a deeper need for connection between people. Ignorance of the "other" is the root problem for animosity between Israelis and Palestinians. Each needs to understand what the other thinks and feels without necessarily agreeing with what is said. I firmly believe that this will reduce the level of violence.

Most of us agree that we need to eliminate hunger, disease, pollution, homelessness, poverty and violence. But we do not agree how this should be done, and the increasing divide between liberal and conservative can be destructive. In some senses Republicans and Democrats follow the poor communication exhibited by the Israelis and Palestinians. While "dialogue" ends up in shouting matches, corruption, unemployment, pollution, violence, hunger and poverty worsen. Too much demonizing results in a circumstance that is devastating. Both can be flawed. The liberals trump the idea of being more "caring," but that blanket attitude often diminishes the poor's potential. The conservatives want a "get-tough" approach, but that also has its drawbacks. It often spells a hard-line ideology that fails to consider the layers of hardship that hold the suffering down. Few are willing to pay the price of collaboration.

Justice has been and can be brought about through interdependence, wherein we are self reliant yet fully responsible to each other. In seeking alternatives, we have the power to eliminate poverty, hunger, crime, racism and many other problems. The question asked by Rebecca Robertson, an experienced city planner, when removing Times Square on 42nd St. in New York was, "Who's willing to 'step up' and remodel something better than what anybody has thought of before?" What she calls "stepping up," I refer to as a willingness to pay the price.[35] A variety of people and organizations responded. Douglas Durst, who initiated the renovation, fought with Robertson for many years, but finally both put aside their biases and prejudices and agreed to build a place of excitement and energy where a million people show up every New Year's eve to see the ball drop. Imagine what would happen in our legislature if our politicians put aside their biases and prejudices, if the achievement at the other end was *justice* rather than a ball drop.

Few fail to acknowledge our overall societal increase in crime, in part because reading statistics causes much pain and heartache and we try to wish away the truth. Consider the increase of prisoners in 1980 from 330,000 to 2 million.[36] How to take action to reverse the trends, however, remains in question. Neither the get-tough or stay-soft approach is the answer. We need to build a society based on strong relationships, preserving the peace rather than just enforcing the law, keeping vigilant concerning the root of our problems rather than

[35] Ibid. p. 299.

[36] Ibid. p. 299.

seeing only its symptoms. More than one right answer is possible. Seeking a better way will produce rich dividends. What if we rewarded people for obeying laws? This approach was applied to a group of teenagers in Canada. They were given a ticket for doing something good, and could redeem it for a slice of pizza, or to go swimming, skating, or golfing, for free. In one instance a teenager saw a small child dash in front of an oncoming car. He immediately snatched the child and saved him, but then saw a policeman approach him. Because he had not heard about receiving a positive ticket, he became fearful and his stomach knotted. He was much relieved to receive a ticket for his heroism. His mother was delighted when she found out the story. This approach has made a dramatic difference in the community.

Our problem in the political realm seems so much more daunting, less easily remedied. The image clogs our collective imagination: Washington is bogged down by branches of polarized partisans incapable of getting much done. In light of the Gordian knot that has become our public policy, direct action is often the best answer. Charities like Feeding America and 91.1 Mix spend the day before Thanksgiving stuffing Milwaukee County buses with nonperishable food. They are given to citizens of southeastern Wisconsin, and have been distributing some 200,000 pounds of food each year for over 15 years. It does not matter whether they are Democrats, Republicans, and Independents. They show how it is possible to work together in Wisconsin, and this charity has been paying the price of unity. In the past, food pantries were used as a safety net. Now they are needed to get people back on their feet which has become far more challenging. In Milwaukee, the Capuchin-run House of Peace and the St. Benedict Center depend on the united efforts of others, and through these combined efforts they have become places that reach out to the poor relieving them of their hunger and their many needs. We might not be united in our politics, but we have to be united to end hunger in our society.

CLIMATE CHANGE

We also need a united effort when alerting others to climate change. The accumulated cost of climate change is becoming more and more imminent. Therefore the price we need to pay to overcome it is also growing. Desmond Tutu maintains that climate change is the moral issue of our time. Many of us talk a lot about being "green," but as a whole we fail to pay the price. What is to be done? We can reduce our fertilizers and thereby improve fuel efficiency of our farm machinery. How much fossil carbon is burned by transporting food around the states? Eating locally is a rather easy practice that significantly reduces this unnecessary consumption. How much energy is used to openly display frozen foods, a phenomenon that results in some people wearing sweaters to go shopping while it is sweltering outside? It is estimated that 40% of food is thrown away or allowed to spoil here in the United States —a wasteful practice that Pope Francis has recently called a "sin." Industrial agriculture could use corn stalks for fuel. Waste biomass, once decomposed, can be used in agriculture instead of diesel fuel which would reduce greenhouse gas emissions. The cost involved is a matter of survival for the human race and a variety of plant form on our earth.

The real victims of climate change are the poor, who are the least responsible but at the same time most vulnerable. We need to question our dependence on fossil fuels which wreak havoc on our earth and threaten the future of our grandchildren. Paying the price of justice would demand that we match the money of oil companies and fossil fuels with our own passion, spirit, and creativity. The fossil fuel industry makes more money than any other on our planet. Exxon and other companies are committed to burning carbon despite the environmental cost because they cannot fathom decreasing their monetary profits. Exxon Mobil spends $100 million a day trying to find more hydrocarbons to burn. They do it by altering the chemistry of our atmosphere, becoming outlaws to the laws of physics by pouring dangerous wastes into our atmosphere. We need to help them become *energy* not *fossil fuel* companies. Responsible stewardship of our planet has to replace fossil fuel dominion. That is the price we need to pay. One way is making sure executives wean our lives off coal, gas and oil. But an even stronger method would be one which ensures that renewable energy does not face an uphill battle. College trustees, pension fund boards and church executives may, in good conscience, resist their fossil fuel stocks. If they don't, we will continue to pay the price of epic drought, arctic melt, and skyrocketing grain prices. Some ironically call America "the exceptional country," because we make ourselves the exception to many rules. Any institution that makes money off of fossil fuels contributes to this destruction. We need to safeguard creation by asking these institutions to sell their stocks and prevent us going down the slippery slope. The irony of our "green," careless position with regard to climate change was illustrated by a bumper sticker on a large SUV which read: "Take care of creation and creation will take care of you." You need a large SUV for those words?[37]

Has climate change become the third rail in politics, much like Social Security? A large majority of people, some 77%, now say that Climate Change should be a high priority for the president and Congress. According to the majority of scientists, Hurricane Sandy is related to climate change. Warmer temperatures lead to water evaporating and more moisture in the air results in catastrophic weather. This is a tough argument to swallow. Bill McKibben, an environmental activist, called Sandy "a wake up call." Climate Change affects all Americans and is an issue vital to our common good. Hurricane Sandy reminded us that climate change is a poverty, race and immigration issue. Poorer communities take longer to recover, being without electricity, heat and water than

[37] Aana Marie, Vigen, and Nancy Tuchman. "Forming in Hell: the New Normal?" *Sojourners.* Vol. 41, No. 10, Nov. 2012, pp. 10-11.

affluent ones. Economic disparity was apparent in New York City, where immigrants lived in constant fear of not being paid for a week because they were non-salaried workers. Pope Emeritus Benedict XVI, like his predecessor Pope John Paul II, emphasises that climate change is not a *political* but a *moral* issue. It is an issue that transcends borders and demands an international response. He and the U.S. bishops warn about the effects climate change will have on future generations, again, especially on the poor. They try to ensure that that industrialized nations develop renewable energy and sustainable economics.

Because it uses so much of the world's resources, the United States plays an important role in climate change advancement. Although the Church does not demand that we take *specific* positions on climate change, we do need to begin to make concrete proposals, so that we take concrete actions. To this end, I believe we should reduce global warming despite the economic costs. A tax on carbon should be imposed. In *The Carbon Crunch* Dieter Helms, a professor at the University of Oxford and a fellow in economics at New College, suggests that this is the price tag involved, because he considers carbon emissions through coal the worst offender. He admits that reigning in carbon emissions is most challenging and maintains that wind, solar and nuclear energy will not meet the world's growing energy needs, a fact corroborated by most environmentalists and energy experts. We need new production techniques, in particular we need a rapid transition from coal to gas, because gas produces only half the emissions. More research is need to develop low-carbon energy and especially solar technologies, even though the latter cannot sufficiently meet the increasing world-demand for energy.

We need to implement cap-and-trade, as well as alternative sources of energy that don't add to greenhouse gas emissions—such as tighter fuel standards for vehicles. Recently, record high temperatures were recorded in Lake Michigan, along with disturbingly lower lake levels there and in Lake Huron. Climate change is real, so Congress and the president need to act before it is too late. Since 2007, an Earth Hour is set aside in March. Participants turn off their lights for 60 minutes as a show of support for tougher action to confront climate change. What if, to show their willingness to pay the price, people did this *every week*?

As cliché as the phrase may be, we still need to reduce, reuse and recycle. The price is worth the efforts. Some simple but effective actions that will help us become more eco-friendly: when shopping take a bag with you; instead of immediately going to a fast food place, put your meals in a freezer to heat and reheat them, which is often healthier; bones from a turkey or chicken can be used for soup; use one-way rags that can be reused or disposed of; recycle cans, paper, plastics, even though this may be inconvenient. Where possible, have a compost heap for coffee grounds and fruit peelings. Extend furniture life by using slip covers which will save us money while salvaging the earth.

BIG MONEY

Another area we need to consider in our affluent society is money. Thomas Jefferson was one of our most brilliant presidents. In the famous declaration we read, "All men are created equal. We are endowed with certain inalienable rights." Do we actually conduct our affairs as if this were true? Money, more than people, has certain inalienable rights, and we are rated by our income. Are we a military empire in which money rules? Pope Francis speaks of this phenomenon as the reign of money with its demonic effects spread through drugs, trafficking, material and moral poverty.

Big money determines who runs for public office, gets elected, and, often how issues are framed. It also robs our nation of having a fair economy and destroys our environment by allowing big companies too much freedom in how they dispose of their waste. Big money controls much of our entire system with tragic results, like people dying because they lack proper health care. Many pharmaceutical companies and insurance industries lobby so they can increase their profits, rather than helping people. We need public interest groups to hold special interest groups in check. How many of our politicians are bought and paid off by big money? Zygl Wilf, owner of the Minnesota Vikings, contributed thousands of dollars to both the Democrats and the Republicans during the 2012 election. He claims to be bipartisan. Doesn't this action suggest, rather, a desire to buy favor with both parties, or a "Buy Partisan" problem? Meaningful campaign finance reform is needed. Are we willing to pay the price of this difficult task, or do we simply say "It is impossible?" The same was said about the abolition of slavery and women's suffrage. Are we willing to pay the price like those who fought against slavery and advocated women's suffrage? Will our economic house get itself in order while there is still a house?

OUR SOLDIERS

Although not one of us could possibly take on all of the tasks I've outlined in this chapter, it is essential that we commit ourselves to redressing some specific social ill(s). If we have problems with "big money," we have even greater ones with our soldiers returning from war. They have certainly paid a heavy price, but they often lose their identity through the ravages of war. Society responds by being oblivious to what these soldiers have endured. They survive, but not some of their buddies. Captain Josh Mantz who served in the Iraq war, saw Marlon Harper die when a bullet penetrated his left arm which severed his aorta. He said that the experience "didn't bring me closer to God." Some soldiers feel the guilt of serving when others die. But moral wounds resulting in post traumatic stress will demand moral healing.

As they enter civilian life, many have lost arms, legs, eyes and other body parts. Some soldiers want to keep these injuries hidden or they refuse to talk about them. Others cannot process what happened on the battle field, or they feel ashamed, and try to cover up any guilt for their buddies' deaths, resulting in an ambivalent attitude toward their own death. Their tragic experiences explain why they have recourse to alcohol or drugs. Still others experience numbness, and as a result many do not care whether they live or die. The numbness can lead to futility, or meaninglessness, and even suicide.

Some soldiers feel morally betrayed. Major Jeff Hall experienced this when he was asked to comfort relatives of a family killed while returning from church. Their car was caught in a cross fire in Baghdad. He assured the survivors that they would receive money to help bury the dead. While enduring endless delays, which resulted in bodies rotting in the summer heat, the family finally received the money: the amount was only $750. The worse indignity came when the death certificates were stamped with **enemy** in bold letters. Hall pleaded in vain to have that changed, and was greeted with a flat refusal. This is another awful example of collateral damage. In the face of this experience, Hall felt more powerless than when he faced enemy fire.

How can we help these soldiers who have paid the price of serving our country? One way is to assure them safe places to talk, whether classrooms or town meetings, open forums where soldiers and civilians might gather to watch documentaries or plays such as "Ajax in Iraq," which has been shown in a number of military and civilian venues. It portrays a parallel story of the soldier AJ, and Sophocles' ancient Greek tragic portrayal of the soldier Ajax. When Major Jeff Hall saw this play, he confessed his shame and admitted to Nancy Sherman, who wrote *The Untold War,* that he nearly committed suicide. Some soldiers inflict a sentence of guilt upon themselves for reasons that are not always just. By talking about their

147

experiences with a professional or a friend, they can better understand that they are not like negligent parents who allowed their child to drown in a pool because of inadvertence.

MEDICAL PROCEDURES

We are finding that some doctors prescribe unnecessary medical tests for their patients. According to Choose Wisely, a foundation focused on encouraging physicians and patients to dialogue about their health and well being, the overused tests for people over fifty, are: EKG's and stress tests, bone scans for osteoporosis for women under 65, and for men under 70, antibiotics for mild and moderate sinus infections, CT scans and other imaging for uncomplicated headaches, dubious diagnostic tests for suspected allergies, X-ray, CT scan and MRI for low back pain.[38] More physicians are warning that the overuse of these procedures cause patients more anxiety, dangerous side effects, pain and even death. Christine K. Cassel, MD, president of the American Board of Internal Medicine maintains that it is important for patients and doctors to talk about treatments that are truly necessary. But are doctors and patients willing to pay the price of their time and efforts?

Sometimes doctors order these tests and treatments to protect themselves from malpractice suits. Patients often demand drugs for ordinary aches and pains.

---

[38] *AARP Bulletin.* May, 2012, Vol 53, No 4, pp. 10-14.

They come to the doctors' offices to be "treated," not to be told they don't "need" a CT scan for a headache. We need to pay the price of advocating that less medicine is often better than more. Too many of us believe that more is better. A recent study indicated that a third of doctors prescribe brand name drugs simply because patients ask for them, simply because they are backed by more advertising and packaging, even though cheaper generics are appropriate. The practice, of course, results in higher health care costs. This was found among doctors who received free drug samples or free food from drug companies, or had financial relations with drug companies.

DEATH PENALTY

The Church stands against the death penalty. Some of the reasons are: 1) it is morally unjust when the state assumes the power to kill someone in the name of the entire community, thereby lowering it to the level of murder; 2) statistics show that it does not deter crime or make our society safer. George Cain, a police officer in Ridgefield, Conn. claimed that if it kept his police and correctional officers safer, he would be for it; 3) it is often applied or even due to the inadequate disproportion to the poor and minorities. One study showed that of the over fifteen hundred executions, only thirty were white people; 4) it is a system that has made a number of mistakes especially when DNA tests have been made, or even the inadequacies of eye witnesses, lab and forensic tests.[39]

One example is Curtis McCarty, who spent 19 of his 22 years in an Oklahoma prison on death row. Three times he was accused of murdering a young woman. McCarty said he was a drug addict but not a murderer. After an investigation conducted by the FBI, investigators found misconduct by the police, prosecutor, and false forensic evidence. He paid the price of these mistakes and false evidence by spending 19 years unjustly in prison.

Presently McCarty lives in Lincoln, Nebraska, and is actively working against capital punishment by giving talks. He has witnessed a man who killed someone in cold blood but who became remorseful, and was led to death wrapped in chains, without any hope of someone to support him. There was nothing he could do, but he knew it was wrong. At one time McCarty considered himself an atheist. But with the help of Sant'Egidio, an Italian movement which places emphasis on outcasts and is recognized by the Church, he now goes to Mass every day when in Rome, and considers himself a Catholic, even though he has not officially joined.

He observes that many Catholics profess that they are Christians but they really are not. They might desire a more profound expression of faith, but many have not read or really digested the Gospels and therefore fail to see how Jesus encouraged us to reach out to the poor, the infirm, and everybody in need. He believes that we need to look at every person, no matter what nationality or creed, as a

---

[39] Winright, Tobias. "Gandalf, Gollum, and the Death Penalty." *Sojourners.* January 2013 p. 23-27

human being loved by God, and help to make their lives better. He feels what he is doing now will help to redeem himself.

Tobias Winright, an associate professor of theological studies at St. Louis University, agrees with the above reasons for not advocating the death penalty, and added another more pragmatic one: the high costs of the states and their taxpayers to implement it. He gives the example of North Carolina, where the state could save eleven million dollars a year by substituting life in prison for the death sentence. Of course, his stance is not supported by mere pragmatics: "As Christians we stand on firm theological, biblical, and practical foundation to announce that the time is now for the U.S. to abolish capital punishment."[40] Richard Viguerie, a conservative icon, believes that there are few things more horrible than innocent people being convicted of crimes and executed. He does not think that Christ would pull the lever to execute somebody, and encourages us to model our lives after Christ.

ADVOCACY

Advocacy means moving out of our comfort zone by helping people who are in immediate need. Are we willing to pay the price of raising the consciousness concerning some injustice? The movie Les Miserables is, in sum, a courageous portrayal of resistance to injustice. Advocacy is a passion to improve other peoples' conditions by changing a structure or a policy. An advocacy group was founded by "Vagina Monologue's" playwright Eve

---

[40] Ibid, p. 23-27

Ensler, to stop violence against women and girls. It is driven by various faith traditions. Because American culture is so action-driven, before acting regarding some injustice, we need to better understand and gather accurate information about the conditions of the injustice. In working for justice we need not work alone.

As Christians, for whom water is an essential symbol, we also need to advocate for clean water and water conservation, another effort that we can share with those who may not share our faith. The average person in the United States uses as much water as 900 Kenyans. Water shortages are becoming more evident in at least 36 states. We can help by eating less meat and switching to a diet rich in vegetables and grains. Steaming vegetables instead of boiling them will entail less water. Supporting small scale family farms who are engaged in sustainable food production. Streamlining the use of water in home gardens and lawns. Native plants require less water. Watering manually is even more challenging, but it saves water. Using rain barrels to water can alleviate the water shortage. We also need to reduce food waste, which recently was estimated at 40%, by buying only what we plan on eating and using left overs in creative ways. How many of us are willing to pay the price involved in accepting these challenges?

We are more concerned about shaping the world than about refining our attitudes toward it. How many of us realize that by taking a strong stand against some injustice like abortion, euthanasia, racism, sexism, and the above mentioned injustices, we become modern day prophets? We might not have to suffer like a Dr. Martin Luther King Jr. or a Bishop Romero, but we will face opposition. Sandra Schneiders helps us to see that Jesus was engaged in a struggle against both social injustice *and* evil that cost him his life. Jesus also warned us that if we are going to be his disciples it will be a costly undertaking. Some of us wear a cross, but are we willing to pay the price to carry it? Sandy's aftermath demands that we as people of faith advocate for holistic justice especially for the poor. Ronald Rolheiser maintains that no one gets to heaven without some kind of recommendation from the poor. If we are to live Christ's life as fully as we can, we must be willing to speak out and act against any injustice. Are we ready to accept Jesus' challenge? If we do accept it, we must not be lacking in hope.

SCRIPTURE PASSAGES FOR REFLECTION

"The poor you will always have with you, but you will not always have me."

(Mt 26:11)

"For I was hungry and gave me food. I was thirsty and you gave me drink, a stranger and you welcomed me."

(Mt. 25:35)

"May all be one, as you, Father, are in me and I in you."

(Mt 17:21)

"For your sakes he became poor, so that by his poverty, you might become rich."

(2 Cor 8:9)

"I urge you, in the name of the Lord Jesus Christ, that all of you agree in what you say, and that there be no divisions among you."

(I Cor 1:10)

QUESTIONS TO CONSIDER

1. What are some ways you might counteract materialism and consumerism?
2. How can you support the poor not just materially but spiritually?
3. How can you become a justice advocate, to eliminate hunger, pollution, homelessness, and violence?
4. What else can you do to become more "green"?
5. How can you help soldiers returning from the war?

CHAPTER EIGHT

HOW HOPEFUL ARE WE?

Thorny justice issues can easily overwhelm us; we need to cultivate hope. It is challenging to believe and hope in our darkest hours that God is there to support us. We remain shocked by the sexual abuse scandal that has haunted us since 1990's, and even more distressed by the fact that many cases stretch even further back in time. We've heard story after story of priests and religious violating their vow of celibacy, as well as negligent bishops being willfully blind to these horrible crimes, and, in some cases, covering them up. These stories continue to show that we are moving through some of our darkest hours as Catholic Christians. Ordinarily, the darkest hour is shortly before dawn. A hope-filled person knows this, and knows as well that behind the darkest clouds there is sunshine to sustain us. Being "hopeful" means being patient, gaining the ability to wait. It means not giving up, even when matters do not get better.

Every day we hear reports of people living in misery, or those who are spiritually poor, because they do not know God. Scientific and technological experiments involving stem cell research and contraceptive pills—including the more recent release of *permanent* birth control pills and over-the-counter abortifacients—surge forward at all costs, with few considering their ethical consequences. Isaiah comforts us in our trials, sharing with us God's words: "When you pass through the water, I will be with you; in the rivers you shall not drown. When you walk through fire, you shall not be burned; the flames shall not consume you" (43: 2). God is there to give us the strength and courage we need to face the future *with hope*. Because we live in an age of darkness and birth pangs, only the hopeful person also sees promise and the possibility of resurrection. Seeds of new hope need to be planted. In an address November 29, 1989, Pope John Paul II encouraged us to build a more just and fraternal world inspired by hope, one that will lead to our greater happiness. All human hope suggests the existence of something grander than what we can imagine. Hope is pregnant with possibilities. Are we willing to pay the price of being attentive to the richness of these possibilities in spite of the darkness around us?

Our tendency is to focus on our problems, trials, difficulties, which only intensifies the pain, and which finally results in more fear and doubt. We become small when we fear, and great when we are hopeful. When we complain about our problems we accomplish little. It is something like spitting in the wind. As we make our journey through life, we encounter hope-filled people who know that difficult or trying events can transform their lives; they teach us that we can find deeper meaning in the difficult things that happens to us. We become much stronger and more loving when we live in hope, because hope is the hub of fresh energy. When Jesus invited Peter to walk on the waters, the disciple was hopeful that he could do this. He was the only one who got out of the boat. But he made a mistake when he took his eyes off of Jesus; his hope, as ours, was contingent on Christ's encouragement. Peter became more concerned about the waves and the possibility that he would sink into the water. The practice of keeping our eyes focused on Jesus produces much hope, and it will prevent us from sinking into fear, doubt and even depression. Jesus assured us that "I am with you always, until the end of the age" (Mt.28:20). Jesus will always be our stabilizing center. Robert Barron brings out this point when he claims that Jesus is "our hope against hope."[41] He also argues that the purpose of the Vatican II was not to modernize the world, but to Christify it. We help to Christify the world by demonstrating that hope born of Jesus, not the false optimism of modernity, is the way to enliven us. It is impossible to avoid all problems and difficulties, but we can ground our hope on the promise that Jesus will not fail us, because he has truly risen. Being hopeful is the price we pay as witnessing to Christ's resurrection. Hope is not cheap, but it is worth paying the price, containing as it does the reality of the resurrection.

We are also hopeful because God loves us unconditionally. The more we grapple with God's love the more hopeful we become. Evangelist Michael Dowd states

---

[41] Barron. *And Now I See*, p.159

that a loving God is the reality that *transcends* and *includes* all realities. Mae West use to say that too much of a good thing is wonderful. This is certainly true concerning God's love for us. Jesus showed us the highest kind of love by suffering, dying on the cross, and rising from the dead, but that love melded with hope in his promise to send us the Spirit. He did not leave us orphans. The Spirit helps us to be hopeful even with regards to our suffering. Suffering has meaning, as we have considered, when we see it in relation to Jesus' suffering. Love will always be stronger than death. Our hope in life is that we will reach our goal of heaven, but are we willing to pay the price of our pilgrimage, especially as we become more aware how interconnected we are?

In *Field of Compassion* Judy Cannato states that "The Universe Story offers us great hope as a species. It is a story that tells us the universe is a single evolutionary process . . . and that all life is fundamentally connected. In this story no one or no thing is excluded from the whole. In fact, the connectedness is so essential that the movement of one part affects the whole."[42] She explains the ways in which the physical and spiritual worlds are intricately connected and offers a message of hope for our troubled times. Once we recognize how interconnected everything is, we may actually become hopeless, because it is overwhelming to think that evil or sin or imbalance in one area can so directly affect another apparently unrelated area. And yet this is precisely the paradox of hope: we

---

[42] Cannato. *Field of Compassion,* pp. 25-26.

maintain it in spite of our circumstances, in spite of the daunting challenges and temptation toward anxiety. All of us can become agents of hope, if we are willing to accept the challenge and price of engagement. Messengers of hope need to fine tune their harps, because one discordant note in a symphony orchestra can disrupt the whole.

A DESIRE FOR FULFILLMENT

Hope always implies a desire that emerges while we expect some sort of fulfillment. What do we desire and want? We never hope for anything we already possess. So, if we have a good marriage, a good job, good health, we can be grateful for these blessings. But if we need a new home, a car, or if we want to win the lottery, we hope to accomplish those desires. Many of us hope we can win the lottery. One man complained to God that he never won a single dollar. After he failed to win several times, and his constant complaints, his wife said to him, "Why don't you buy a ticket?" If we are hopeful we cannot afford to sit on our hands, but be willing to pay the price of our efforts. How many of us would consider fishing as a ritual of hope? When fishing, we have to be watchful and alert to the slightest touch on the line. We hope that a fish might take the bait or lure. If our concentration diminishes, even for a second, we might miss what we hope to catch. Fishing helps us to better comprehend Jesus' command that we stay awake!

Writing to the Romans Paul expresses his greeting in terms of hope: "May the God of hope fill you with all joy and peace in believing, so that you may abound in hope by the power of the Holy Spirit" (15:13). God is the source and giver of this grace, and unceasingly encourages us to be hopeful and joyful. Joy, peace and hope are intimately connected. When we consider the first of these virtues, we are speaking not of a worldly, but a spiritual joy. Hope is grounded on what God sees in us, not what we are able to accomplish. Jeremiah states it well: "For I know well the plans I have in mind for you, says the Lord, plans for your welfare, not for woe! Plans to give you a future full of hope" (29:11). God will help us to accomplish our plans in proportion to our capacity to hope, just as God helped Jeremiah accomplish his task of warning the people to repent even when he faced extraordinary resistance.

The symbol of hope has always been an anchor. It has saved many a ship tossed about like a toy on the stormy sea. Once the anchor grabs the sea floor, it promises safety for everyone on the ship. We are often tossed around by the waves of doubt, fear, and discouragement. As we embrace the future, we need the anchor and stability of hope. Hope assures us of a bright future, despite the difficulties and hardships we might encounter. Hope enables an artist to envision what he might draw or paint on an empty canvas. We are future-oriented, as Pierre Teilhard Chardin contended, and often filled with great expectations of what might happen. But a gap always exists in what we possess, what we hope for, and the price we are willing to pay. Bridging that gap means we have to hug or cuddle the ambiguity and uncertainty of the future with an evergreen hope in our hearts.

Ladislas Orsy notes that if we hope, there is no gap, because hope fuses the present and the future. The kingdom of God has already come. We already carry the future in our hearts; we experienced the "already and the not yet." Our difficulty is that we seek after worldly goods, driven by a strictly human, earthbound hope. We need to be unfettered by the influence of consumerism, especially in the United States. Becoming unbound is costly. Divine hope seeks after heavenly gifts. As St. Paul states, "If then you were raised with Christ, seek what is above" (Col 3:10). We don't rely on our own strength, but the grace of the Holy Spirit who invites us to seek a world of hope and meaning, where our basic needs—first and foremost our need to be loved—are met. The Holy Spirit can release torrents of hope on our parched planet and on us, if we allow the Spirit to grab us by our lapels. Once we place our hope, happiness and joy in our future, eternal life, all falls into its proper place. It is the very nature of the Holy Spirit to do something new, to surprise us, by drawing us deeper into our relationship with God and others.

HOPE AND CHANGE

Hope also means that we are open to change. *Hope* and *change* were the key words of the 2008 election for Barack Obama. But much of the hope projected onto the president has faded. For reasons already touched on, we still have not solved our deepest problems: we lack political cooperation; special interest groups have great power; under Obama, as under so many presidents of recent date, uncivil partisan warfare rages; unlimited expenditures mar political campaigns, (because of a Supreme Court ruling). Our system is, overall, broken. Many elected politicians had hoped to change all this. Money still has a choke hold on our democratic process, a dysfunction that works against all those who are powerless; any hope we place in political institutions must be measured.

In a certain sense, having hope in the promise of the resurrection is even easier than having hope in the future of democracy. In *Christianophobia: A Faith Under Attack* Rupert Shortt argues that the virtue of hope will be needed in large doses if Christians are to face and survive the persecution they are enduring. Many have paid the price with their lives: they gave us hope in the afterlife by themselves loving the life to come more than their own heartbeats. Hope is God's steady hand on the rudder, guiding us through rough waters toward our goal.

As we journey, a spiritual choice exists: do we move toward cynicism or toward hope? Hope breaks apart the scabs of cynicism, guiding us in all our decisions and actions. Are we willing to pay the price? It is easier to be cynical. It costs less, at least initially: the price we pay for it in the end is immense. *Sojourners* is working to embody hope through a recently launched project called "Emerging Voices," through which they want to develop and promote the most dynamic speakers, preachers, and teachers to articulate the necessity of social justice. What we need today are not more saviors, but more prophets. Mother Teresa, Dorothy Day, Mahatma Gandhi, Dr. Martin Luther King Jr. were prophets not saviors. Their hope was not in their own powers. This is crucial because there is a danger in placing the wrong kind of trust in one person. We place our trust and hope in Jesus, who will never disappoint us.

We still need more people of hope to inspire us, a "great cloud of witnesses," to steer us in the right direction (Heb 12:1). We need to become agents of change, not dragging our feet, but putting our foot on the gas pedal—looking to the future. In the future, and in many senses even now, whites will and do not have a racial or ethnic majority. The aim of *Sojourners* is not to evoke a single voice, but a number of voices, who can instill hope into the social justice challenges that we face as a nation. Pope John Paul II wrote, "A sign of hope is the increasing recognition that the dignity of human life must never be taken away, even in the case of someone who has done great evil."[43]

PEOPLE OF HOPE

Pope Emeritus Benedict XVI is a pope of hope. His messages are hope-filled, especially his encyclical *Spe Salvi* (on hope), in which he teaches us that Christianity needs to offer a transformative hope that goes beyond

---

[43] Winright. "Gandalf, Gollum, and the Death Penalty," p. 27.

human effort or vague spiritualities. Hope has to transform us from the inside out, otherwise our hopes will be easily shattered—like a dropped, thin-rimmed glass. Hope can be shattered by the choices we face in life. When we encounter doubts, fears, and worries, hope will prevent us from a spiritual meltdown.

Sargent Shriver was a man of hope. President John F. Kennedy asked him to take over the Peace Corps, which was destined to find its end in the waste bin. He had to weigh the cost of this challenge, because there was no funding available and much opposition from significant foreign agencies. President Eisenhower dubbed it a "juvenile experiment." Despite all the odds against it, all the noise that claimed it would not succeed, Shriver—who went through laborious months of lobbying, appearing on "Meet the Press," and appealing to youth—was able to establish the Peace Corps on a sound basis. Shriver's hope drove him further, and he didn't stop there. He also fought against established discriminatory practices in the Chicago area, only to have bricks thrown his office windows.

Nevertheless, Shriver marched on. He established Head Start, Legal Services, Vista, and the Special Olympics in 1984. He persisted in convincing China to join the Olympics, which it did in 2007. Through many of his speeches he had the ability to inspire people to do something about poverty, racial injustice, or any of the other burning issues at the time. He told the Yale graduates to break their mirrors, to look less at themselves and more to others and their needs. Alzheimers forced him to resign from the Olympic World Summer Games. Remaining upbeat, he faced a new challenge with much

165

grace. Shriver was asked by his son (during one of his lucid moments) how he felt about losing his mind. He responded, "I'm doing the best I can with what God has given me."[44] Mark also acknowledged that his father might have felt disappointed, but that he did not let it linger or turn into anger. He noted that his father believed God was in control, even when he lost his bid to become president and vice president. Shriver was truly a man who did not lose hope.

Anyone who ever met Sister Thea Bowman has recognized immediately that she was a woman of hope. She was asked to give the keynote address to a national gathering of Bishops in 1989, at Seton Hall University in South Orange. Sister Thea told them what it meant to be black in our church and society. She came before them to represent her community's hopes and struggles, a community she referred to as a "motherless child." When she came to church, she came "fully functioning," which meant that she was present with all she had and hoped to become. She hoped that all people could walk together as a family, instead of being separated into, black and white, clergy and laity, men and women. Crossing these lines is price we need to pay, she insisted, so that we can overcome poverty, loneliness, alienation, and so that people will know that we love one another. Sister Thea held the bishops spellbound. When she finished, she asked them to sing "We Shall Overcome," which they did.[45]

---

[44] Mark, Shriver. *A Good Man*. New York, NY; Henry Holt, 2012, p. 190.

[45] More found in Roberts, Tom. *The Emerging Church*. pp. 2-6.

In a 2009 talk, Marti Jewel, a professor at the University of Dallas who has studied the shifts in Church leadership, said that "Pastoral leaders are living into the new realities that face them. There is a palpable sense of longing for hope and support. In that hope they can call on the words of the U.S. Bishops themselves, who have recognized some of the shifts under way." Such a mutual support can only exist if each side is able to authentically hope in the other. One of those shifts is the need of mutual support between clergy and laity. Imagine what could happen when clergy and laity combine their efforts in confronting our common problems.[46]

Ms. Aung San Sui Kyi, a 66 year old democracy activist, overcame difficult hardships to receive the Nobel Prize at Oslo, Norway. In 1991 many thought that she would never be able to deliver her speech for winning the prize. As a Myanmar opposition leader, she was honored as a hero in Washington, D.C. on September 17, 2012, by both John McCain and Hilary Clinton. She is like Nelson Mandela, who never gave up hope even when he spent fifteen years in detention. Now, in large part due to the efforts of Aung San Sui Kyi, the political reality changed in remarkable ways. International pressure accomplished her release from house arrest in 2010, which inaugurated a new beginning for Burma during a very critical time of dictatorship to democracy. Her hope is to bring peace as leader of the opposition party in Parliament by working with her former military captors. Because they hold a

---

[46] Ibid. p. 37.

quarter of the seats in the legislature, Ms. Aung San Sui Kyi is willing to compromise with them "without regarding it as humiliation." She acknowledges that the road will not be smooth, and will cost the people many twists and turns as they overcome the many obstacles. What an example for our own deep divisions in the United States. She has become an icon and is idolized by Bono, because she hopefully engages in the messy business of negotiation.

Cesar Chavez was willing to risk giving up his job at a Community Service Organization, where he conducted voter registration, in order to protest police brutality. He turned down a job from Sargent Shriver to head the Peace Corps in various Latin American countries. His wife Helen had to work in the fields so they could support the family, while he crisscrossed San Joaquin Valley, talking to farm workers, trying to instill in them a sense of hope. The agricultural business was based on cheap labor that treated them more like farm machinery than human beings. But he had hope in something larger than himself, in the promise of God's justice.

He visited many of his *compesinos* who told him that to organize a union was impossible. Money, law, and history were against him. But hope inspired him, at the age of 35, in September, 1962, to start a National Farm Workers Association in Fresno, California. Cesar knew it would take several years before they could organize a strike. Meanwhile, the Agricultural Workers Organization Committee started their own grape strike. What were they to do, watch from the sidelines or join them? They chose the latter.

The two organizations eventually united to form the United Farm Workers Organization with Cesar as its head. Governor Ronald Reagan called them "barbarians," ordering prison inmates and welfare recipients to replace them. The California Supreme Court struck down the ruling. Images of President Richard Nixon eating grapes were broadcast on national TV, and the United States Department of Defense bought three million pounds more than before. The crowning act came in July 1970, when the farm growers and the farm labor union signed a contract.

Despite many setbacks, failures and shortcomings, Cesar was a man deeply rooted in hope and in his Catholic faith. He attributed his faith to his mother and Reverend Donald McDonnell, who helped him understand the papal encyclicals. He also cited St. Francis of Assisi and Gandhi. Christ became the center of his life, especially motivating his message about feeding the hungry, clothing the naked. He spoke about his lengthy hours thinning lettuce, as a time when he felt as if he was nailed to his cross. When his associates turned against him, the Eucharist became his source of strength and hope. Daily Mass was most important to him, as was a devotion to Mary under the title of Our Lady of Guadalupe. Finally, short fasts also were part of his spiritual menu. It is easy to see that his hope came from a deep well, a divine well. He died in San Luis, Arizona, on April 23, 1993, but his spirit lives on in the United Farm Workers. Barack Obama borrowed his slogans for his campaign, "*Si, Se Puede!* Yes, We Can!"[47]

---

[47] Hedick, Barry. "Cesar's Choice," *America*. Vol 207 No 5, August 27, 2012, pp. 15-18.

Spencer West was diagnosed with a rare genetic disease and lost both of his legs. The doctors told him that he would never be able to function in our society. But West proved them wrong by climbing the 20,000 foot Mount Kilimanjaro with his hands at the age of thirty-one in 2012. Two friends accompanied him. At times they carried him and at others he used a wheelchair. His hope never wavered, and he accomplished his goal in seven days.

He did it to raise money for Free the Children, an organization that is dedicated to building schools in Africa. But West did not consider himself as a sign of hope to others as he traveled around Africa. During his climb, he saw stone structures which are called cairns. They are a symbol for anyone who is lost, helping them to find the trail again. He considered himself a cairn. He now hopes others will be inspired to overcome any challenge as he did.

SUICIDE

Some people live on the opposite end of the spectrum. Unlike Shriver, Chavez, Aung San Sui Kyi, or Spencer, they find life meaningless and give up hope. Their lives may even end in suicide. Losing a loved one through suicide is troubling and costly experience. We need to console and comfort survivors as they endure their bereavement. Good and solid material on this subject is scarce. When someone we love commits suicide, we live with much pain and often guilt, wondering what we could have done to prevent this. We ask, "How is God going to treat this person?"

The tendency toward suicide is often caused by a disease, much like alcoholism. We probably will never understand why people take their own lives, especially if they are religious, or there were no signs of suicidal tendencies. We need to guard against spending much time and psychic energy trying to figure out what we could have done to prevent this deed. Since it is an illness, much like cancer, we often are unable to save the person. God loved this person even more than we did, but did not interfere with her or his freedom (if we can indeed say that such a person was *free*). I remember when my niece committed suicide, and the effect this had on my sister. What complicated the situation was my inability to attend the funeral because of a prior commitment which could not be canceled. I felt so helpless, because I wanted to be there to console her and preside at the funeral.

Above all, we need to put aside our anxiety and stop worrying over how God will handle this situation. As in a certain sense our prayers are outside of time, we can pray with confidence for those who have taken their lives —even many years after the fact. God's immernse love cannot compare to our love for the person. Ronald Rohlheiser believes that most people who commit suicide will find Christ waiting for them with open arms saying, "Peace be with you." Some people fail to make a distinction between killing oneself and suicide. We might know of someone who was not an egoist, a narcissist, a proud person, but nevertheless took her and his own life. Hitler and many others like him also killed themselves. An infinite distance exists between the two, and our God is most merciful and loving to those who takes their own lives.

Simone Weil thought of committing suicide at the age of fourteen, after having experienced a spiritual crisis, which was brought on by severe migraine headaches and her own unworthiness. After receiving her degree in philosophy at the Sorbonne in 1931, she actively worked to bring about justice, especially for the oppressed. She even took a position in a car factory in order to better write a book on labor. This activity and her own deep faith and hope enabled her to deal with her suicidal tendencies.

Dakota Meyer believed he did not deserve a Medal of Honor. While in Ganjgal, Afghanistan, he heard that his fellow marines were pinned down. He risked his life while locating four dead soldiers who were stripped of their gear. Meyer had taken seriously the mandate "leave no man behind." One year later on September 8, 2009, however, he wanted to take his own life, finding his struggles with loneliness and leading a normal life unbearable. Taking a gun from his truck's glove compartment, he pulled the trigger. But someone had removed the bullets. He still does not know who did it. Meyer sought treatment for post-traumatic stress. He still feels that the medal memorialized the worst day of his life, but he is still here. We need to work to instill hope in those have endured traumas such as Meyers.[48]

Our hope is not based on a distant God, but grounded on the words of Jesus who dwelt among us: "I am with you always, until the end of the age" (Mt. 28:20). As hope-filled people we do not avoid bristled problems, but embrace them as Jesus did, with the assurance that he will be with us as our solid ground on which to stand.

---

[48] Found in *Into the Fire: A Firsthand Account of the Most Extraordinary Battle in the Afghan War.*

SCRIPTURE PASSAGES FOR REFLECTION

"For I know well the plans I have in mind for you, says the Lord, plans for your welfare, not for woe! Plans to give you a future full of hope."

(Jer 29:11)

"When you pass through the water, I will be with you; in rivers you shall not drown."

(Is. 43:2)

"I am with you always, until the end of the age."

(Mt 28:20)

"May the God of hope fill you with all joy and peace in believing, so that you may abound in hope."

(Rom 15:13)

"Hope does not disappoint."

(Rom 5:5)

QUESTIONS TO CONSIDER

1. What do you desire and hope for?
2. Are you open to change and hopeful for the future?
3. How does hope help you to counteract doubts, fears, worries?
4. Of the people of hope in this chapter who inspires you the most?
5. What can you do to assist those for whom life has become meaningless?

CHAPTER NINE
REACHING OUT TO OTHERS

The Buddhists have an expression, "It is our turn to help the world." An artist needs to step away from his painting to gain perspective. We need to do the same, otherwise all we see is violence, hatred, murders. Unless we step back we will not even believe it *possible* to help others in need. It is challenging to see God's presence in the ordinary raw experiences of life. Belief has to begin with ourselves. If we cannot believe in the miracle we are, how can we believe in the miracle that created us? Good starts with us, right here, right now. We have a responsibility to reach out to others who cry out to us like a siren in the night. For the most part we hurry, because we are so empty. Too much turning inward, however, cuts us off from the source of our strength. We need to concentrate on what is good in every situation, in every person, no matter how tragic and trying. That will enable us to be thankful and become more alive and vital. As the psalmist said, "At dusk weeping comes for the night; but at dawn there is rejoicing" (30:6). When we are clothed with love we can rejoice even in darkness. It takes much courage to laugh at the power of darkness. Did you ever notice how often children laugh in contrast to adults? Some say five hundred times a day: we, maybe three. We need to be childlike in the face of darkness.

In an important sense we are taught today to be more careful than carefree. Even though we cannot provide food for *all* the hungry, reach out to *all* the poor, we can still live differently in order to reach out to *some*—and that some will be changed. The question remains, how can we loosen our grip on material goods? We die a little to conventional ideas of richness and freedom to become more authentic. Redemption comes from walking through the pain, not avoiding it. It is said that God walks in two shoes, the shoe of creation and the shoe of the incarnation.

Jesus warns us in the parable of the talents about the price we have to pay for burying our talents. We can easily bury them by giving into unjust anger, resentment, jealousy and hurts, rather than taking the risks necessary to share them, to put them at the service of the common good.

There is a price to be paid for allowing these emotions to control us, rather than using the energy to reach out to others. We become restless, upset, and lose our peace of mind. This phenomenon can occur in the most ordinary situations. I know of a woman who became so angry at one of her friends because she did not pick her up at the airport that she decided not to call her on her birthday. She later regretted her initial response, and called her. Challenging tasks, such as letting go of our hurts, or whatever negative emotion it may be, makes us feel uncomfortable, and we would rather avoid them.

Resentment comes from a Latin word "sentire" which means to feel. Put the "re" in front of it, and resentment means to feel the hurt, insult, or whatever it may be, again. Some cannot let go of their hurts and keep on rehashing them, which results in a buildup of the resentment. Letting go of hurts is challenging, but it can be done in the context of prayer and spiritual guidance. How willing are we to pay the price? The alternative is pricey in another way. As Augustine teaches us, resentment is something like hoping another person will die after we ourselves ingest poison.

The story is told of a student who came to her master and asked, "What is the difference between one who has wisdom and knowledge and someone who is enlightened?" The teacher responded, "The one who has wisdom and knowledge is the one who carries a candle in the darkness and lights the way. The one is enlightened has become the torch itself."[49] Which are we, one who carries the torch, or the torch itself? St. Paul was a torch, even as he was thrown out of the best of synagogues. He suffered many hardships, but continued to preach and teach. We are also called to share responsibility with God for the good of others, and that is no small task, especially when we face opposition to our ideals and convictions. J.K, Rowling, the author of the *Harry Potter* series, at one time was penniless, depressed, divorced, and trying to raise a child while attending school. Today she is one of the richest women in the world because of her hard work and determination. She certainly faced challenges, but did not

---

[49] Edith, Prendergast, RSC. *Grace Abounds*. Notre Dame, IN; Ave Maria Press, 2011, p.57.

allow them to become the center of her life, and turned outward to the world through her fiction.

If we are going to reach out to others, we need resilience. Most of us experience this as we bounce back from hard times, pressures, and stress. At times we can feel like we are crushed in a vice. Resilient people, however, have the ability to cope with these situations and live happier, healthier and longer lives. Recovering alcoholics, drug addicts, binge and compulsive eaters, can help others who have similar problems, because they are willing to pay the price of dealing with their own addictions.

According to St. Paul, a Christian is someone committed to dying and rising with Jesus. Very few of us, if any, will die the way Jesus did, but all of us are invited to imitate his psychological suffering. In Christ this suffering is always endured *on behalf of someone else or something greater than ourselves.* This can consist in the pain and death of giving ourselves for others. Despite rejection, nothing could prevent Jesus from showing his love to others. Even though Jesus was abandoned by his Apostles, he continued to give of himself. He was concerned for others even those involved in his death. He returns the high priest's servant's ear. He tells the women not to weep for him but for themselves and their children. He forgave those who nailed him to the cross because they did not know what they were doing. St. Paul encourages us to imitate Jesus by giving of ourselves completely to others, "Have among yourselves the same attitude that is also in Christ Jesus" (Phil 2:5). Pope Francis insists that a church which refuses to go out of itself will soon sicken from the stale air of its closed rooms. We might, he said, have "accidents," as we "go outside," but he prefers that to a sick church.

When called by Jesus to reach out to others, we need to respond in the first person: "Yes, I will do it," not in the second person, "You should do it," or in the third person, "He or she should do it." Otherwise, we act like a couch potato quarterback, always eager to explain in detail how others need to respond. Some of us might respond like Isaiah and say we have unclean lips, or like Paul who said that at one time he persecuted the church, or Peter who declared that he was a sinful man. We have to realize that God knew them better, and knows us better, than we know ourselves. God takes the weak and limited, as Paul found out, and transforms them into people of boundless courage and bravery.

WHAT AM I GOING TO GET OUT OF IT?

We are all familiar with the expression, "What am I going to get out of it?" and it points to a difference that exists between getting and giving. Many people came to Jesus to be healed, as the evangelist Mark points out: "They laid the sick in the marketplaces and begged him that they might touch only the tassel on his cloak; and as many touched it were healed" (6:56). They came to Jesus to get something, to be healed. Nicodemus came to Jesus at night to get something, even as he also was then able to bring the spices for Jesus' burial. Zacchaeus wanted to get something, to see Jesus, and so he climbed a sycamore tree. But he also gave Jesus a meal, and he and his household converted. We might look upon Jesus in these situations as a bell-hop in a hotel, but are we willing to pay the price of giving of ourselves to those who are in much greater need than we are? Mary Magdalen did not count the cost of anointing Jesus' feet with precious oil. It was an honor to anoint someone's head. As the psalmist says to the Lord, "You anoint my head with oil" (23:5). She did not consider herself good enough to anoint his head. She was even willing to unbind her hair, which typically signified an immoral woman. And yet the whole house was filled with the fragrance. Interpreting this moment in the Gospels, the Fathers of the Church see the fragrance of the Good News as spreading throughout the whole Church. Notice that perfume, something entirely non-human, became the source of truth. We can turn to God's creation to find answers and healing that cannot come from other people. One of the Fathers of the Church, St. John Chrysostom, maintained that bees are worthy of honor, not because they work hard, but because they labor for others. In the Christian tradition, bees are associated as symbolizing cooperation and diligence, good virtues for reaching out to others. St. Theresa of Avila believed that bees can teach us much about the prayer of quiet, wherein we enjoy a peaceful union with God. She observed how if no bees entered the hive, and if none attempted to bring others in, they would not produce much honey. Pope Pius XII wrote that bees work together without envy or rivalry. This trait holds true in human beings who are outward looking, but also demands a price. Givers tend to be happier people, a fact which was brought out by an experiment where one group of people was given money to spend on themselves, and another group was to spend it on others. Guess which group was the happiest? Helping others in need can also have a similar effect.

Rodney Stark, a sociologist, points out that the mutual help given by the early Christians to one another in times of plague, fires, floods, and other natural disasters, affected their survival rate, as can be seen when we compare them to pagan citizens. Outsiders were deeply impressed and attracted by this outpouring of aid. St. John Chrysostom encouraged Christians to advance in good works and please Jesus the Savior. In reaching out to others, Pope Francis insists that we must maintain an interior oil of joy that can transform our hearts.

The last words that eight year-old Jayden Lamb spoke before he died of cancer were, "God needs me more." But those words changed a community. As a symbolic gesture to thank the community for all they did to support the family during the two and a half year ordeal, his folks decided to pay for the customer behind them at a drive-through. A chain reaction began in Midland, Michigan. In honor of Jayden, a diamond ring was put into a Salvation Army kettle, a waitress was totally surprised to receive a $50 tip, restaurant owners were shocked to find that customers were paying for others' meals. To top it off, when Jayden's parents ate at a restaurant, they found that their bill was already paid.

These are examples of "Pass it On," or the willingness to pay the price for someone else's kindness.

The 2012 Synod in Rome emphasized that we need to reach out to those who have no faith or have become "tired" of their faith. Parishes, or movements intimately connected with them, need to extend the welcome mat. How many are willing to pay the price of reaching out to a mobile society, where people shift their allegiances with a blink of an eye. And yet we need to reach out beyond our own parish, especially to those who no longer practice their faith. The Synod insisted that we are all in this together. We cannot pretend this mobility, this constant shifting, does not exist, or pretend that we are not all interconnected.

Introverts find it difficult to reach out to others in typical, publicly-oriented ways. They often resist the invitations to help in highly social settings. Extroverts reach out in public more naturally, and easily overcome most obstacles to helping others. Introverts will often avoid people or look the other way, and are content with just a few friends. Extroverts are just the opposite. If introverts can reach out to one person rather than making many contacts, it might alleviate their fears. Introverts can often give depth that extroverts cannot access because their strengths lie elsewhere—often in action. If they invite someone to their home, they might have to set a clear closing time ahead of time, because some people have a tendency to linger. Introverts can also give to others in introverted ways, by, for instance, doing tasks that require less interaction but still serve the common good.

181

COMMON GOOD

Loving and reaching out to our neighbor, a Gospel principle enunciated by Jesus, serves the common good. Enacting a commitment to the common good will either surprise others (in those cases where narcissism or individualism has taken full root) or attract others to do likewise. Some people brag when they reach out to others that they have God on their side. Abraham Lincoln's greatest concern was not whether God was "on our side," but whether the people of the United States were on God's side. That might mean changing our outlook, and put aside our revengeful, petty politics. We need to reach out and set our moral compass on the hungry, the poor, the lonely, and the outcasts of our society. Preoccupation with pettiness is a malady among some, something which prevents them from having new experiences, which can demand a price of their time and talent. Preoccupation keeps things the same, and it is a sign we are paralyzed by fear and uncertainty, and that phantoms take precedence over the greater needs of others. The Good Samaritan story shows how easy it is for people to find excuses that explain away why they cannot help others. *Who is my neighbor?* remains a burning question. It needs to be answered with concrete action and risk-taking.

Christianity was never meant to offer a free ticket to heaven. Rather, it consists of a challenging call to relate more intimately with *God* and *others*, especially those who are in most need of our help: the poor and vulnerable. All world religions agree that these two relationships—with

God, first, and with others—are closely connected. This dynamic force will improve our society and our world. We need to fight not just for our own narrow rights and privileges, but for policies that will meet the rights and needs of all. In order to rise from our often fragmented social order to achieve a common end, basic questions need to be asked: how do we work together even with people with whom we don't agree? Are we committed to reaching out to the poor and vulnerable, even if we disagree on various philosophical, political, or theological grounds? How do we put others first, and not become overly concerned about ourselves?

Jorge Mario Bergolio, before he became Pope Francis, is a good example of someone who dreamed of a missionary church. A missionary church is one in which members constantly strive to forget themselves. Bergolio embodied a church that was very concerned about people whom he considered to be on an "existential garbage pile." After his election he continues to dream of a "poor church for the poor," calling the universal Church to put its most precious resources at the service of those who have least.

Jim Wallis believes a commitment to the common good, which lays the foundation for common ground with others, is necessary if we are to carry out the greatest commandment. He wonders if we as a country will move in the direction of looking out more for ourselves, or if something will prompt us to redirect into one that promotes the common good. Solidarity is a Gospel principle totally embraced by Catholic social teaching. The fact that one out of three Americans live below or near the poverty line demands a response from us. Working poor and middle class families are desperately trying to make ends meet, while white collar executives earn huge salaries. Our faith urges us to help the poor lift themselves out of poverty. We also have a responsibility to remind the government of their responsibility. Jesus declared it, "You shall love the Lord, your God, with all your heart, with all your soul, and with all your mind. This is the greatest and the first commandment. The second is like it: You shall love your neighbor as yourself" (Mt. 22:37-39). Many stories are told of how people of faith who had the common good in mind reached out to the victims of hurricane Sandy and the Boston Marathon. But are we willing to pay the price of reaching out to others on a daily basis without some kind of tragedy provoking us? If we are attentive enough, we will see that "tragedy" is a daily reality for many; by meditating on those whose lives are fraught with crosses, we can attune ourselves to them when we see them throughout the day. Better yet, we can place ourselves in their midst.

PEOPLE WHO GIVE OF THEMSELVES

L'Arche is a community reaching out to the "least of these," a community in which the least are put first, in this case the people with special needs. Putting them first goes contrary to what our society teaches, as people who are mentally or physically challenged are not likely to make the next profitable gadget or increase "progress." It is not an easy path and carries a price tag. People with intellectual disabilities move slowly, and we live in a fast and frantically moving society. Much patience is needed. Ministers at L'Arche learn how to slow down and appreciate everyone and everything around them, which means that they must dismantle their barriers and their prejudices.

Betty Gerstein, an eighty-year old woman who lives in Delray Beach, Florida declares that, "Everything I do is free." She volunteers at the Delray International Tennis Championships, witnessing some of the greatest pros, enjoying a free breakfast and lunch every day. She helps out at the Downtown Boca Film Festival and is rewarded with free movies. She ushers at *The Nutcracker* ballet for three weeks, and helps the Chamber of Commerce, which provides lunch every day. Gerstein volunteers for numerous events at Lynn University in nearby Boca Raton. She estimates that 70% of her time is spent in volunteering and believes those who live such lives have more fun.

In *The Third Alternative* Stephen Covey states, "It is my personal belief that we are on this earth to serve others, that God expects us to do His work by helping our fellow men and women."[50] He also contends that we might be the answer to someone else's prayer for help and that service to others is the key to lasting happiness, as well as the measure of true success in this life. If we help only

---

[50] Covey. *The 3rd Alternative*, p.429.

when we feel like it, we need not pay such a price, but devotedly caring for others involves a whole new level of giving, a whole new cost.

Argentinian and Catholic layman Juan Carr is a veterinarian, and social entrepreneur who established the "Solidarity Network." Once the torrential rains and vast floods hit Argentina in 2013, killing more than 50 people, Carr was willing to pay the price and moved into action. He drove a large red truck to the cathedral in Buenos Aires, where Pope Francis used to offer Mass. (Carr was and remains Francis' staunch backer). Carr collected food, clothes and various other kinds of supplies for the victims. "Solidarity Network" has some 800 volunteers and at least 38 offices set up in the country. The outpouring for the victims has been unbelievable, and he attributes it to Pope Francis and his reputation to reach out to the poor. He calls this generosity the "Pope effect." Juan has noticed a split between the spiritual side of the Church and those committed to social issues. He believes that Pope Francis has the unique ability to combine the two. Carr was nominated for the Nobel Peace Prize in 2012.

In Kathmandu, which is Nepal's capital, women who commit a crime are sent to prison with their children so that the young ones don't try to survive out on the street. When Pushpa Basnet visited this prison, she was deeply touched by the children and wanted to reach out to them. She was even moved to pay the price of starting a home for them. Many believed it would not be possible, and others laughed at her. Basnet's day care center has grown into what is called "Butterfly Home," and it takes care of 40 children. Once mothers give her permission, she takes them in, but she also tries to keep the children connected with their parents by various visits. She feels blessed to have these precious children spend time with her.

Sarah Berg, a nurse assistant, was traveling by car in Menominee, Wisconsin area, when a flat tire stranded her. Victor Giesbrecht and his wife, who were traveling from Canada were on same road, and pulled over to help her. Once Victor had changed the tire, he and his wife continued on their trip, when suddenly, he felt a heart attack coming on and steered over to the side of the road. His wife got out of the car and waved frantically for someone to stop. Sarah who was traveling on the same highway, saw her and, as a Good Samaritan, immediately pulled over and administered CPR. If she had not stopped to help him, Victor would have died. Her training in nursing helped her to act as quickly as she did. What a powerful story of reverse roles, of people being willing to pay the price of helping one another.

A similar incident happened to Mark Hirtreiter in February 2012, while he traveled on U.S. 41 near West Bend, Wisconsin. He missed his exit and then saw a car that was in trouble. He did not know that the occupant had passed out because of a medical condition, and had crashed his car into a guard rail, which caused the engine to ignite. A number of motorists stopped and were valiantly trying to smash the windows of the car to get the man out. Fortunately, Hirtreiter had a fire extinguisher, which enabled him to run across the highway to help the others. All of them worked diligently together to save the man from dying. They were able to extinguish the fire and pulled the man to safety before the 911 personnel arrived. Mark did not claim to be a hero, but did what needed to be done. He claimed that it is a natural tendency to help someone who is in real trouble no matter what the cost involved.

Father Solanus Casey, OFM Cap, believed that we can help others even in a trifling way by sweeping the floor, pulling weeds, picking potato bugs, or a word of sympathy. He quoted Michelangelo, "Trifles make perfection and perfection is never a trifle"[51] He was not afraid to write to someone, encouraging the individual to come down from their "high horse of haughtiness." A very wise man, Father Solanus knew that we would meet gentle breezes as well as Hell-storms in life, but "by the grace of God, we shall be able to tumble into our graves with the confidence of tired children into their places of peaceful slumber."[52]

Edwarda O'Bara spent forty-two years in a coma in her Miami Gardens home. In 1970, she fell ill and slipped into a diabetic loss of consciousness. She told her mother Kaye before slipping into unconsciousness, never to leave her side. She never did. She was willing to pay the price of turning her every two hours to prevent bedsores and feeding her through a tube. Kaye's husband died in 1976, and he maintained that her daughter was a blessing

[51] Bernadine, Casey, SNJM. *Letters from Solanus Casey.* Detroit, MI; The Solanus Guild, 2000, p. 96.
[52] Ibid. pp. 98-99.

not a burden, regardless of the mounting bills. Kaye, a devout Catholic, could feel the presence of the Blessed Mother in her daughter's bedroom. Wayne Dyer was so impressed with Kaye, that he wrote a book about her willingness to pay the cost of unconditional love and what her example might teach us. When Kaye died in 2006, her sister Colleen quit her job and took care of Edwarda. Colleen claimed that Edwarda was the best sister in the world, as she taught her so much about unconditional love and patience, which she said was lacking in her own life. As Colleen put it, this experience helped her to grow up overnight, This story illustrates well what Ilia Delia, using a quote from St. Paul reminds us that "Eye has not seen, nor ear heard what God has prepared for those who love without counting the cost" (I Cor 2:9). "It is a love that seeks justice and peace . . . a love that will result in a new earth and heaven."[53]

In *A Knock at the Door* Wayne Bisek tells the story of how his family had very little at Christmas: an absent father, not enough for a good meal, and only a few presents because his mother scraped together enough money. One Christmas, however, there was a knock at the front door. When Wayne opened it, he found "Booby" Kostner, the owner of the local Farmer Store with bags of bread, meat, fruit and ice cream. That incident changed his life, and now he is willing to pay the price by involving himself in Buckets for Hunger, which, through fundraising events, has established many centers throughout the United States feeding thousands of people.

---

[53] Delio. *The Emerging Christ*, p.137.

According to many surveys, ministry to others can enhance our spiritual growth even if it takes a toll on us. People who don't minister to others are less satisfied with their spiritual growth. Through helping others we often discover even more of our gifts. By accepting Jesus,' "Go and do likewise," we come to know him better, others, and ourselves. Church communities can become stronger by reaching out to others, whether comforting those who mourn, sharing food with the hungry, or providing shelter for the poor. Jesus said, "Be merciful, just as your Father is merciful" (Lk 6:36).

We are given a choice, not *whether* we can choose to serve, but what form our service will take. We can respond to some local need through service at a food pantry, a shelter for the homeless, or by serving hot meals, as community members do six out of seven nights per week at St. Benedict's in Milwaukee, Wisconsin, a Capuchin community. All these projects are meant to build up the body of Christ, as Paul exhorted the Ephesians (4:12). Mother Teresa reminded us that there are no great deeds. Rather, there are small ones which are done out of tremendous love.

SCRIPTURE PASSAGES FOR REFLECTION

"They laid the sick in the marketplaces and begged him that they might touch only the tassel on his cloak; and as many touch it were healed."

(Mk 6:56)

"You shall love the Lord, your God, with all your heart, with all your soul, with all your mind. This is the greatest and first commandment. The second is like it: You shall love your neighbor as yourself."

(Mt 22:37-39)

"Who is my neighbor?" "Go and do likewise."

(Lk 10, 29, 37)

"Eye has not seen, and ear has not heard, and what has not entered the human heart, what God has prepared for those who love God."

(I Cor 2:9)

"Go into the whole world and proclaim the gospel to every creature."

(Mk 16:15)

QUESTIONS TO CONSIDER

1. How willing are you to reach out to the poor, the vulnerable, the outcasts of our society?
2. How can you work with people who disagree with you?
3. What helps you to put others first rather than yourself?
4. What prevents you from sharing your faith with others?
5. Can you get involved in a project that serves others?

CHAPTER TEN
CHALLENGE OF DAILY PRAYER

One of the objections to daily prayer that I hear most is, "I am overworked and too busy." In an overstimulated, overworked world, praying daily is another cost of being a Christian. Certainly parents raising children, or those holding down two jobs might not have sufficient time. Henri Nouwen described our lives rather vividly when he compared them to over-packed suitcases. If a suitcase is over fifty pounds at an airport, we have to pay extra money. I have seen a number of people transferring some items to another suitcase, to get under the fifty pound limit, or, better yet, discarding some of their unnecessary belongings. If only we could do that with our work or daily tasks. Many feel as though they are working inside of a pressure cooker. People in such a condition often see prayer as one thing to add to their to-do list, as another chore among many others.

If we are too busy to pray, David Henry Thoreau asks, what are we busy about? We find time for television, reading the newspaper, eating, sleeping, and many other things. We can so easily become involved in a whirlpool of activities, a careless crisis which Thomas Merton considers an act of violence against ourselves. Our monthly planners contain little-to-no unscheduled blocks. Someone showed me her planner recently and I was amazed to see how jammed packed it was. And this was without scheduled slots of prayer!

Jesus also led a busy life, as recorded in Mark's Gospel, "People were coming and going in great numbers, and they had no opportunity even to eat." Jesus suddenly said to the Apostles, "Come away by yourselves to a deserted place and rest a while. So they went off in a boat by themselves to a deserted place" (6:31-32). The Apostles became more aware that Jesus was drawing his strength, courage, and wisdom from his prayer life. We find Jesus in prayer in at least fourteen passages in Luke's Gospel. If he prayed, then how much more should we ourselves—we who are *not* God? Realizing their ignorance, the Apostles asked him to teach them how to pray. He taught them how to be grounded in something beyond themselves and their selfish ambitions. How often we are taken up with our plans, projects, and problems. Jesus said, "Where your treasure is, there also will your heart be" (Mt. 6:21). What do we think about most? We can become very self-centered, like the publican in the temple who thanked God he was not like the rest of humanity. Jesus taught the Apostles the Our Father with the challenge, "forgive us our sins for we ourselves forgive everyone in debt to us" (Lk 11:4). In the Acts we read that Stephen was a prayerful man, filled with the Spirit, and he was willing to pay the price of his life. While being stoned to death he said, "Lord, do not hold this sin against them" (Acts 7:60).

Prayer helps us to pay the price of forgiving others who might have hurt us, and also to forgive ourselves of past offenses.

Our to-do lists, like are planners, never seems to diminish. We always have one more thing to do: bills to pay, items to be picked up at the store or mall. All the hours in the day are insufficient to accomplish all that "needs" to be done. Our work can consume us or we can use it as an escape hatch that helps us not to face some harsh realities we might encounter. We rush around answering cell phone messages, checking and sending e-mails, making appointments. Even when immersed in our work, we can feel homeless, especially when we stand at the crossroads of mobility. Old maps no longer work for us. Our fast-paced lives add to our struggles, and leave us unbalanced and restless. Life is too fast and fragile. We need to slow down and listen to God's whisper, so we can walk with awareness and soft steps, to allow all of nature to touch us deeply.

Pope Francis encouraged us to stop and take the time to talk with the Lord during the day. But we don't want to slow down and pray, because that means facing ourselves, or entering into deeper relationships, especially with God. Besides, there is a price to be paid if we want to follow through on this adventure. If we are unwilling to pay the price, however, we begin to descend down the slippery slope of disaster. The Greeks insisted that our greatest conquest is ourselves. Alexander the Great was an outstanding soldier. One day, in a fit of rage, he killed one of his closest friends. Here was a man who conquered all the known world of his time—but he could not conquer himself. Are we willing to pay the price of conquering ourselves? We cannot do so without praying.

Prayer is a doorway into silence. The letters of the word "silent" can be rearranged to spell out "listen." We will miss much in life when we refuse to pay attention or listen in prayer. When we listen, prayer becomes a search. Mary and Joseph had to search for Jesus until they found him in the temple. Prayer is a consecration and also a letting go of all human relationships. Jesus said to John from the cross, "Woman, behold your son" (Jn 19:26). His perfect prayer prepared him to let go of everything, even his mother. Prayer embodies a thirst to deepen our relationship with God. Jesus cried out on the cross, "I thirst" (Jn 19:28). Prayer is a handing over of our spirit, discouraged and broken as it is at times. Our prayers need not exclude our brokenness. Jesus said, "It is finished. And bowing his head, he handed over the spirit" (Jn 19:30). Sometimes prayer is a running to the tomb of the Lord, only to find emptiness: "They both ran, but the other disciple ran faster than Peter and arrived at the tomb first; he bent down and saw the burial cloths there, but did not go in" (Jn 20:4-5). Prayer is simultaneously a call by name and a letting go. Jesus called Mary by name, but also said, "Stop holding on to me, for I have not yet ascended to the Father" (Jn 20:17). Prayer is receiving the Holy Spirit. Jesus breathed on the Apostles and said to them, "Receive the Holy Spirit" (Jn 20:22).

We often think that we initiate prayer. It is hard to believe that God seeks us, an alternative phenomenon which the poem, "Hound of Heaven" enunciates: "I fled Him, down the nights and down the days."[54] God wants intimacy with us, which at first we might find frightening. Henri Nouwen speaks of prayer as soul work; souls are sacred centers where God is with us in an intimate way. That is why I always consider it a privilege to help people in spiritual direction or a directed retreat. I have come to appreciate that they are inviting me into the library of their souls, trusting me with many pages that are very sacred.

We are told to take time to smell the flowers, but the flowers of our prayer life can wilt or even die. We could refer to our teetering economy as an economic thrombosis. What about a spiritual thrombosis in prayer? We experience this when we are afraid to deal with the deeper issues of our lives, especially our relationships, using the lame excuse that is the mantra of this chapter: we are too busy. Society might even praise us because we are eager beavers who get things done. Work, however, can become an addiction; we become workaholics. Do we ever hear of people sent to clinics for prayerlessness? Alcoholics and drug addicts are sent there, but not those who don't pray. And yet addiction to the material world, a world without prayer, is often a grave problem.

Some find their meaning in life by indulging in too much work instead of working to strengthen their

[54] Thompson, Francis. "Hound of Heaven." http://www.ewtn.com/library/HUMANITY/ HNDHVN.HTM. 5/13/13

relationships. Choosing the former can cause a tectonic shift, producing much stress in our lives. But the great spiritual writers point out that if we emphasize more our relationships, especially with God in prayer, we will find our true meaning and values in life. Jesus had to point this out to Martha when she complained about having to prepare the meal, while Mary sat and listened to Jesus. Jesus does not chastise her, because he repeats her name, which is a sign of affection. He helped her to realize that, under these circumstances, Mary had chosen the better part. From our own experience, we know that there are more important things than work.

Prayer has to become a priority in our lives. If we are to grow spiritually, we need a disciplined prayer life. Discipline means making a decision to pray every day, and then sticking to that decision. I walk every day, but there are days when I don't feel like walking, because of weather conditions, or because I suffer aches or pain. But I try to discipline myself to do it. St. Paul insists that we need to be "self controlled" (Titus 1:8). To be self controlled we have to pay the price of a disciplined prayer life, a time to read and meditate on the Scriptures.

IMPORTANCE OF MEDITATION

Studies have shown that meditation is a way to inner wisdom, a new consciousness. Those who are faint of heart or weak in spirit will experience meditation as very challenging. We will often face our shadow, become aware of our inconsistencies and our selfishness. Meditation can teach us that we are not our thoughts, feelings, or even our daily experiences. It helps us not to judge our initial shortcomings in this practice, but to allow events to unfold knowing that God is still in control. Some days we need to give up other "activities" in order to pay the price to meditate; we need to persevere in our efforts. In this way, meditation will teach us that God is present in all the events in our lives and in the world.

Our prayer will improve when we find a balance between the left and right brain, leading us to seeing anew how God is present in the world. Bill Harris of Centerpointe Research Institute believes that meditation can help eliminate lateralization, a condition in which either the left or right brain dominate. Various methods, like repeating a mantra, looking at a candle, or deep breathing, help to synchronize and connect the two brains. If we are willing to pay the price of daily meditation, the rewards are abundant. First and foremost, our spirits grow. We also learn to relax and be less stressed. In a sense, a rewiring results in our becoming who we really are.

Meditation is living the present moment, the now, not the future or the past. We become more present to God, ourselves, others, and the world. We are opened to our addictions or dysfunctions, and are willing to embrace them in a way that rejects their dominance or control. Daily meditation allows us to become better Christians, and even beyond that, a saint, if we are willing to pay the price. But we have a strong desire to be in control, rather than in the "hands of the uncontrollable."[55] What needs to follow is a spirit of "let come," as Judy Cannato points out, an attitude which puts the focus on letting *come* whatever is there, something quite different from the letting *go* process.[56] Both are challenging, and we have to pay the price if we want our prayer life to grow. It has been proven that people who attend services more than once a week live seven years longer than those who don't. They also are less likely to indulge in drugs, alcohol, and are satisfied with less money. Belonging to a faith community of prayer will also increase our happiness.

NEED FOR DAILY PRAYER

Pope John Paul II told us that as a child he would wake up sometimes at night to find his father on his knees praying. He called his father "Captain," a Captain who encouraged him to pray daily, which inspired Karol to think of life as vocational. Thomas Keating believed that the only way we can fail in prayer is not to show up. In *Be A Man!* Father Larry Richards states, "Pray. The more we pray, the more we open ourselves to the glory of God. The less we pray, the less we will grow in holiness."[57]St. John Vianney was sent to Ars, France, to a very small parish out in the sticks— because he was not very bright. But he spent whole nights in prayer which resulted in passionate sermons. Even kings and queens of France came to hear

---

[55] Cannato, Judy, *Field of Compassion*, p. 203.

[56] Ibid. p. 123.

[57] Richards. *Be A Man!* p. 169.

him. He felt that his responsibility was to pray and love. Henri Nouwen speaks of prayer as a dedicated vocation. The saints certainly made prayer their vocation. We need prayer because most of us are challenged with hectic schedules, which easily tax our patience and lead to tiredness and even exhaustion. Prayer can become a life and death situation for some of us. In the most self-interested sense, we need prayer to steady our shaky lives and connect us to divine energy, so we can carry out our daily tasks. By means of prayer we can work even more profoundly on behalf of the common good. Without prayer we will not be energized to carry out our daily tasks. What struck me about reading the life of Mother Teresa is that she was bursting with so much energy, despite all the sufferings she endured. She readily admitted, however, that her energy came from God in prayer, not from herself. She was willing to pay the price of taking time for her prayer.

Anthropologists point out to us that no matter what our religious affiliation, contact with a deity is of utmost importance. One sign of a healthy Christian is consciousness of our desperate need for prayer. But, we might ask, why should we pray, if God already knows what we need? Why bother or waste God's time? One reason is we might more easily delve into our deepest feelings and longings. Another reason: prayer is a two-way street between ourselves and God, who wants to communicate with us more than we realize. Here is the risk: we might have to change our way of thinking, acting, or our attitudes. We resist change as we have considered. As one poster put it, "The only person who welcomes change is a wet baby." Through spiritual direction and in conducting directed retreats, I have experienced how individuals change their lives once they immerse themselves deeply in prayer and are willing to pay the price of accepting change.

Deacon Tom Lambert of Chicago, who co-chairs the National Catholic Partnership on Disability's Council on Mental Illness, admits that his faith was a crucial element that helped him deal with his daughter's mental illness. He learned to turn things over to the Lord in prayer, which has helped him immensely. He suggests that people with mental illness be remembered in the Universal Prayer at Mass, especially considering that they are often overlooked. Sometimes the best pathway into prayer is not to pray for ourselves, but for others, as this experience will draw us out of ourselves into God's divine love.

DISTRACTIONS

How often I hear from directees, "I have so many distractions in prayer." Distractions in prayer can often upset us. They might be compared to what Robert Frost described as having a lover's spat with the world. Our distractions in prayer can be a sort of lover's spat, because they often discourage us. Thank goodness our distractions are not sledgehammer or jack hammer noises in the background. But other noises can distract us, especially when we focus on them. A couple of dogs in the backyard of a home two doors north of us often bark during our meditation period from 4:45 to 5:15 P.M. They can easily upset me. At other times, we can be distracted by endless words or mental chatter. If a plane is flying low and the sound is rather loud, instead of getting bothered I say a prayer for the pilot and passengers, so they will reach their destiny safely. When distracted, we might also choose a mantra, a word, or phrase that is meaningful to us, one that will bring us back into a deeper praying space. Attending to one's breathing is also helpful. The inhaling and exhaling might move us beyond word or thought.

Another way to deal with distractions is to focus on centering prayer, which can be very challenging in the beginning. But we need to persevere, and be willing to pay the price for our efforts. Father Walter Ciszek, S.J., was able to persevere in prayer as he was fire-tested in Moscow's dreadful Lubyanka prison. He turned his five year solitary confinement into a school of prayer. Growth in prayer will usually entail a purification process. Ciszek experienced much powerlessness through being cut off from everything, especially those who could help him. He maintained that his faith in prayer sustained and allowed him to become more God-conscious while deepening his relationship with God—this in spite of the fact—that he suffered from fear, insecurity and depression. His prayer aided his ongoing conversion, and his perseverance counteracted his loneliness and confusion. Despite the fact that he felt hopeless, he immersed himself in a prayer where he experienced "total blackness" turning into a "blinding light." This caused him to abandon himself completely into God's hands.

He often recited the psalm "My times are in your hands; rescue me from my enemies" (31:16). He realized that willpower was not so important as presence and an awareness of God which helped to dispel his doubts. Ciszek learned a spirit of prayer, courage, and deep trust in God. The silence was conducive for his prayer. While in prison, he more fully realized Jesus' words: "Behold, I am sending you like sheep in the midst of wolves" (Mt. 10:16).

Once he was released from prison, however, his spirit of recollection faltered. He became more distracted by different realities of life, and was challenged to listen more intently to his inner conscience which invited him to abandon himself totally to God's will. His journey in prayer is closely related to many of the saints.[58]

Some expect that when praying they will be so connected with God that they should *feel, sense,* or come to know something profound every time. Trouble looms if that is our approach. The more we pray, the more we become aware of our distractions, and the more we can detach from what is least important to our spiritual lives.

PRAYERS NOT HEARD

The objection I hear often about prayer is, "I pray, I pray, and I pray, but God does not answer my prayer." Jeremiah assures us, "When you call to me, when you go to pray to me, I will listen to you" (29:12). When we pray for what we want and God does not grant our request, our

---

[58] John, Levko S.J. "Chained but Free," *America.* Vol. 208, No 1, January 7-14, 2013, pp. 19-22.

natural response is to become upset or angry. This is not prayer, but a way to use God for our own purposes. Can we be grateful even when God does not grant our request? Some of the saints would compare their lack of a prayer response to eternity. Jesus prayed for Peter, as well as for us, "that your own faith may not fail" (Lk 22:31). Peter's faith did fail him, but can we say that Jesus' prayer was not heard? We need to pay the price of not always having our prayer requests granted.

Several times in the Gospel Jesus said, "Ask and it will be given to you" (Mt 7:7). Often people interpret this passage to mean that whatever we ask from God will be granted, which is a basic tenet of the prosperity gospel. This passage is not a blanket promise that all our requests will be answered. Many of my petitions have not been granted, and I am sure you would say the same. But the prayer might be answered in some other way, such as gift of more patience, or an openness to *allow God to be God*, as the saying goes. It takes much faith to realize that our request might not be answered in the way we hoped it will be. Who knows what is best for us, God or ourselves? What is the saying? "Be careful what you pray for." Every request needs to be accompanied by the words Jesus prayed in the garden, "Not my will but yours be done" (Lk 22:42). In this way we pay the price of praying for what God wants, not what we want.

To put it in another way, we do not pray to obtain results, because at times there aren't any. Can we be okay with that? At the center of every prayer we should ask that we become able to love God and others. We pray to become a better people, the people God is calling us to be. Our "best selves." We gradually become these people, but shouldn't expect it to happen overnight. We have instant coffee, tea, and interest, but there is no instant spirituality. The real test is to persevere in our prayer the way Monica did with her son, Augustine. Or the woman who asked me, "How long do you think I prayed for the conversion of my son?' I asked, "how long?" "Forty years," she responded, "before he finally converted." One of the secrets of all prayer is perseverance, and that is the price we have to pay.

In *Pilate's Prisoner: A Passion Play,* when Lucius, Pilate's slave, was dying and not healed, Jesus says, "I've prayed for things before that were not granted, yet that hasn't diminished my belief in the power of prayer. I continue to pray with confidence because God, being compassionate, only grants what is good for us and for those for whom we pray."[59]

A DYING AND RISING IN JESUS

Prayer is also a dying and rising in Jesus, who made it very clear that we have to lose our life to save it. Ronald Rolheiser states that we have to be willing to die a little since Jesus was willing to die for us. One of the central demands is that we die to our selfishness, our unjust anger, resentment, jealousy, grudges, hurts, and lack of forgiveness. This can be painful, like staying in the

[59] Edward Hays, *Pilate's Prisoner: A Passion Play.* Bradenton, FL; Booklocker, 2012, p.179.

tomb for three days, when we desire to come out after one day. Many of our hurts are excess baggage that we carry through life and we need to lighten our load. The best advice I received when traveling abroad was to travel light. I could understand why, when I saw people toting their heavy luggage from buses to trains. By hanging onto our hurts we remain bound like Lazarus, and need to let go as we hear the words of Jesus to the man proclaimed dead, "Untie him and let him go" (Jn 11:44).

Prayer is a question and a search. "Pilate said to [Jesus], what is truth" (Jn 18:38)? Truth itself was standing before him, and he failed to recognize it. Prayer is the awareness that Jesus is the man and God. "Pilate said, behold the man" (Jn 19:5). Do we recognize Jesus as truth and how prayer has helped us to recognize Jesus as the man-God? Have we ever found prayer a consecration of our human loves while we yet experience the distance? Do we thirst for a deeper prayer life as Jesus thirsted on the cross? Prayer is knowing ourselves better because through the resurrection we discover that God is our Father. Jesus said, "Go to my brothers and tell them, I am going to my Father and your Father, to my God and your God" (Jn 20:17). Engaging in prayer means opening ourselves to a mission. Jesus said, "Peace be with you. As the Father has sent me, so I send you" (Jn 20:21). Prayer should enable us to bring the good news to others. Prayer can ever encompass and then triumph over doubt, and then say the overwhelming "My Lord and my God" (Jn 20:28)! We can doubt that we are able to reach out to others, so we need to answer the question Jesus asked of Peter, "Do you love me more than these" (Jn 21:15)? If our answer is "Yes,

Lord I love you," we will need to alter our actions (Jn 21:15). We will feed his lambs, feed his sheep, reach out to others, despite the price we have to pay.

What enabled Mother Teresa to reach out to the poorest of the poor, cleaning them, watching them die in her arms? It was her dedication to her prayer life, even though often she felt nothing. But she continued to spend an hour before the Blessed Sacrament or say the rosary, especially before she had an interview with some reporter.

CONTEMPLATION

Pope Francis stated that if we listen to the Lord we will learn to contemplate. Pope Emeritus Benedict XVI has encouraged us to use the ancient practice of prayerfully reflecting or meditating on the Scriptures, a process known as *Lectio divina* ("holy reading"). This process can lead to contemplation. After forty two years of itinerant ministry, Richard Rohr decided to devote his life to contemplative prayer. He now teaches contemplation through webcasts and is involved in the Living School for Action and Contemplation. His hope is that contemplation will enable people to become more compassionate, loving, joyful, and as part of the fruits of this, they will engage in social action.

Contemplation means being more passive than active, living out the prayer of simplicity, wherein we concentrate on God's presence. We end up loving more and thinking less, as St. Therese Lisieux encouraged us to do. Moses was certainly awed by the burning bush, which was not consumed. We can be awed by the way in which God bursts through our very beings but does not consume us. We can be awed by a beautiful sunrise or sunset. Thomas Merton was certainly lost in contemplation at 4th and Walnut St. in Louisville, Kentucky, when he suddenly became aware of God loving all these people around him. He was overwhelmed that he also loved them, that they were united with him and were no longer strangers. Merton experienced such joy that he laughed out loud. He found this experience impossible to explain.

Reflecting on God's Word can lead us into contemplation, provided that we don't take the words apart to find out if we agree or disagree with them or give way to other heavily analytical attitudes. Sometimes we must simply allow them to penetrate our inmost being, even to the corners of our heart where they have not yet reached. Nevertheless, we can easily become disturbed and find contemplation useless, because we are just "sitting there," or "doing nothing." We need silence, because it is the best way to respond to the Word. In silence we learn how this kind of prayer will deepen our awareness of God's presence in our lives. Entering more deeply into God's intimacy, we will learn to embrace our suffering, which helps us to become more loving people. Love and pain *can* coexist. This coexistence became evident for the Apostles on Mt. Tabor as well as in the Garden. We too, have our Mt. Tabor as well as our Gethsemane experiences. By praying we can begin to recognize the rhythm of Christ's life in our own.

Prayer will always remain the mystery of God's loving relationship with us. We will struggle, trying to remain faithful to daily prayer as we continue to wade through distractions, through the difficulties of "unheard prayers," and through spiritual dryness. If we are willing to accept these challenges, prayer will transform our lives and we will fulfill the meaning of the word "Christian," becoming more like Christ because we have paid the price of daily prayer.

SCRIPTURE PASSAGES FOR REFLECTION

"When you call on me, when you go to pray to me, I will listen to you."

(Jer 29:12)

"Ask and it will be given to you."

(Mt 7:7)

"Where your treasure is, there also will your heart be."

(Mt. 6:21)

"Jesus said to them, come away by yourselves to a deserted place and rest a while. People were coming and going in great numbers, and they had no opportunity to eat."

(Mk 6: 31)

"Not my will but yours be done."

(Lk 22:47)

QUESTIONS TO CONSIDER

1. What prevents you from daily prayer?
2. Do you find it hard to forgive others or yourself?
3. Why do you find it hard to slow down or be silent?
4. Are you afraid of intimacy with God or others?
5. What method of prayer do you find helpful?
6. How do you respond to distractions or unanswered prayers?

BIBLIOGRAPHY

Allen, John. *A People of Hope.* New York, NY; Image Books, 2012.

Barron, Robert. *And Now I See. . . A Theology of Transformation.* New York, NY; Crossroad, 1998.

Breton, Le Binka. *The Greatest Gift.* New York; NY Doubleday, 2008.

Bushlack, Thomas. "The Age of Skepticism," *America.* Vol. 208, Vol. 4, Feb. 11, 2013.

Callewaert. Joseph, *The World of St. Paul.* Trans. Michael Miller, San Francisco, CA; St. Ignatius Press, 2011.

Cannato, Judy. *Field of Compassion.* Notre Dame, Indiana; Sorin Books, 2010.

Casey, Sister Bernadine. *Letters from Solanus Casey OFM Cap.* Detroit, MI; The Father Solanus Guild, 2000.

Covey, Stephen. *The Third Alternative.* New York, NY; Free Press, 2011.

Dear, John. *Lazurus, Come Forth.* Maryknoll, NY; Orbis, 2011.

Delio, Ilia. *The Emerging Christ.* Maryknoll, NY; Orbis Books, 2011.

Dunn, James. *Jesus Call to Discipleship.* New York, NY; Cambridge University Press, 1992.

Eppinga, Joanie. "The Face of Hate," *Sojourners.* Vol. 41, No 6, June, 2012.

Garvey, John. *Modern Spirituality.* Springfield, Illinois; Template, 1985.

Griffin, Emile. *Green Leaves for Later Years.* Downers Grover, IL; InterVarsity Press, 2012.

Groenings, James. S.J. *The Passion of Jesus and Its Hidden Meaning*. Rockford, Illinois; Tan Books and Publishers, 1928.

Hays, Edward. *Pilate's Prisoner: A Passion Play*. Bradenton, FL; Booklocker, 2012.

Helm, Dieter. *Carbon Crunch*. New Haven CT; Yale University Press, 2012.

Hermes, Kathryn. *Beginning Contemplative Prayer*. Cincinnati, OH; Servant Books, 2001.

Hershey Terry. *The Power of Pause*. Chicago, Il; Loyola Press, 2009.

House, Silas. "Singing the Stories Untold," *Sojourners*. Vol. 41, No 11, Dec. 2012.

Hudock, Barry. "Cesar's Choice," *America*. Vol. 207, No 5, August 27, 2012.

Hugo, William. OFM Cap. *Studying the Life of St. Francis of Assisi*, 2nd ed. Hyde Park, NY; New City Press, 2011.

Levko, John, S.J. "Chained but Free," *America*. Vol. 208, No 1, January 7-14, 2013.

Luntz, Frank. *Words that Work*. New York, NY; Fine Communications, 2000.

Massingale, Bryan. *Racial Justice and the Catholic Church*. Maryknoll, NY; Orbis, 2010.

O'Brien, David. "Change in the Church," *America*. Vol. 207, No 4, August, 13, 2012.

Patterson, Kerry. Joseph Grenny, Ron McMillan, and Al Switzler, *Crucial Conversations*. New York, NY; McGraw Hill, 2012

Pendergast, Edith. RSC *Grace Abounds*. Notre Dame, IN; Ave Maria Press, 2011.

Perrota, Louise. *All You Really Need to Know About Prayer You Can Learn from the Poor.* Ann Arbor, MI; Servant Books, 1996.

Pope Benedict XVI. *Jesus of Nazareth: The Infancy Narratives,* Trans. Philip Whitmore, New York, NY; Image Books, 2012.

Richards, Larry. *Be A Man!* San Francisco, CA; Ignatius Press, 2009.

Roberts, Thomas. *The Emerging Catholic Church.* Maryknoll, NY; Orbis, 2011.

Sherman, Nancy. "Hidden Wounds," *America.* Vol. 205, No 17, May 21, 2012.

Shortt, Rupert. *Christianophobia: Faith Under Attack.* New York, NY; Random House,

Shriver, Mark. *A Good Man.* New York, NY; Henry Holt Company, 2012.

Theissen, Gerd. *The Shadow of the Galilean.* Minneapolis, MN; Fortress Press, 2007.

Thompson, Mark and Nancy Gibbs. "The Insidious Enemy" *Time.* Vol. 180, No. 4, July 23, 2012.

Trudeau, Kevin. *Natural Cures Revealed.* Westmont, Il; Alliance Publishing Group, 2006.

Vigen, Aana Marie and Nancy Tuchman. "Farming in Hell: The New Normal?" *Sojourners.* Vol. 41, No 10, November 2012.

Viguerie, Richard. "Who Would Jesus Execute?" *Sojourners.* Vol. 42, No 1, January, 2013.

Wills, Gary. *Why Priests? A Failed Tradition.* New York, NY; Viking Penguin, 2013.

Winright, Tobias. "Gandalf, Gollum, and the Death Penalty," *Sojourners.* Vol. 42, No I, January, 2013.

Wright, N.T. *Christians at the Cross.* Ijamsville, Maryland; The Word Among Us Press, 2007.

15915054R00130

Made in the USA
San Bernardino, CA
12 October 2014